# ORGANIZATIONAL ASSESSMENT AND IMPROVEMENT IN THE PUBLIC SECTOR WORKBOOK

*Advancing excellence*
*in public service . . .*

# American Society for Public Administration
# Book Series on Public Administration & Public Policy

## David H. Rosenbloom, Ph.D.
### Editor in Chief

**Mission:** Throughout its history, ASPA has sought to be true to its founding principles of promoting scholarship and professionalism within the public service. The ASPA Book Series on Public Administration and Public Policy publishes books that increase national and international interest for public administration and which discuss practical or cutting edge topics in engaging ways of interest to practitioners, policy makers, and those concerned with bringing scholarship to the practice of public administration.

## RECENT PUBLICATIONS

### Organizational Assessment and Improvement
### in the Public Sector Workbook
by Kathleen M. Immordino

### Challenges in City Management: A Case Study Approach
by Becky J. Starnes

### Local Economic Development and the Environment:
### Finding Common Ground
by Susan M. Opp and Jeffery L. Osgood, Jr.

### Case Studies in Disaster Response and Emergency Management
by Nicolas A. Valcik and Paul E. Tracy

### Debating Public Administration:
### Management Challenges, Choices, and Opportunities
by Robert F. Durant and Jennifer R.S. Durant

### Effective Non-Profit Management:
### Context, Concepts, and Competencies
by Shamima Ahmed

### Environmental Decision-Making in Context: A Toolbox
by Chad J. McGuire

### Government Performance and Results:
### An Evaluation of GPRA's First Decade
by Jerry Ellig, Maurice McTigue, and Henry Wray

American Society for Public Administration
Series in Public Administration and Public Policy

*Advancing excellence in public service . . .*

# ORGANIZATIONAL ASSESSMENT AND IMPROVEMENT IN THE PUBLIC SECTOR WORKBOOK

## KATHLEEN M. IMMORDINO

Routledge
Taylor & Francis Group
New York  London

First published 2014 by CRC Press

Published 2019 by Routledge
711 Third Avenue, New York, NY, 10017
2 Park Square, Milton Park, Abingdon, Oxon OX14 4RN

© 2014 by Taylor & Francis Group, LLC
*Routledge is an imprint of the Taylor & Francis Group, an informa business*

International Standard Book Number-13: 978-1-4665-7994-1 (Paperback)

---

### Library of Congress Cataloging-in-Publication Data

---

Immordino, Kathleen M.
  Organizational assessment and improvement in the public sector workbook / Kathleen M. Immordino.
    pages cm. -- (American Society for Public Administration book series on public administration &
    public policy)
  Includes bibliographical references and index.
  ISBN 978-1-4665-7994-1 (pbk.)
   1. Organizational effectiveness--United States--Evaluation. 2. Administrative agencies--United
States--Management--Evaluation. I. Title.

JK421.I523 2013
352.3'75--dc23                                                                           2013016489

---

**Visit the Taylor & Francis Web site at**
**http://www.taylorandfrancis.com**

# Contents

# Acknowledgments

This workbook, like the original book on which it is based (CRC Press, 2010), owes a great deal to Dr. Brent Ruben and the Center for Organizational Development and Leadership at Rutgers, The State University of New Jersey. Dr. Ruben developed *Excellence in Higher Education* (EHE) (NACUBO, 2009), an adaptation of the Baldrige National Quality Award Criteria for higher education, which is, in many ways, the inspiration for what became the Public Sector Assessment and Improvement model. EHE showed that it was possible to customize the language and culture of the Baldrige criteria to meet a specific, narrower portion of a sector. As a doctoral student working with Dr. Ruben, I had the opportunity to see, first hand, the difference that can be made when the participants in an assessment program are comfortable with the language and the examples being used. My many discussions with him about assessment contributed much to the end product. In that same way, I owe thanks to the Baldrige National Quality Award for its long history of promoting and facilitating assessment in organizations. I consider this book to be a supplement to the excellent work that the group does and applaud the steps taken to bring formal assessment processes to the public sector.

I also would like to acknowledge the leadership and staff of the New Jersey Department of Transportation, who participated in both a department-wide Baldrige assessment in 2000, and in the first tests of the Public Sector Assessment and Improvement model in 2004. Their comments and feedback helped a great deal in refining the model. Thanks go especially to my former colleagues in the office of the Assistant Commissioner for Administration and its divisions: Bonnie Zanolini, Janice DeJohn, Sandra Furness, Gregory Vida, Alfred Brenner, and Eileen Fitzpatrick. Thanks go, as well, to my colleagues at Rutgers University, whose insights have deepened my understanding of the practical application of organizational assessment: Brent Ruben, Sherrie Tromp, and Barbara Corso. Thanks to Patricia

Worthington and John Dourgarian for their thoughtful review and comments on the manuscript.

I also am grateful to the American Society for Public Administration for its continuous support of all public sector professionals, and for developing this book series. Dr. Evan Berman graciously served as editor for the original book and supported the proposal for the workbook. A special note of thanks belongs to the late Warren Barclay, ASPA member and public servant extraordinaire, whose encouragement made the original book possible.

Lara Zoble and Amy Blalock at Taylor & Francis Group have been invaluable in working with me through the process of producing this workbook. I sincerely appreciate the support of everyone at Taylor & Francis who understood the potential of this workbook to reach practitioners at all levels of government.

As always, the greatest thanks must go to my husband (and fellow government administrator), Howard Immordino, and to my children, Matthew and Jaclyn, for their constant support and encouragement.

# Introduction

Organizations of all kinds, in order to remain effective, must continuously improve themselves in response to the challenges confronting them. Those in the public sector are no exception. Government agencies at all levels are subject to both internal and external pressures that result in frequent—some would say, constant—pressure for change. New constituents and beneficiaries, new programs or funding sources, new expectations and technologies all mean new approaches and reorganized priorities.

At the same time that the scope of services provided by government is growing, the critics of government agencies are becoming more vocal about what they perceive to be the agencies' problems, including waste, cumbersome bureaucracies, and resistance to change. Internally, the push to evaluate performance and improve services comes from elected and appointed leaders as well as career managers and staff who are trying to stretch limited resources. In order to make resources available for both existing services and new challenges, they must continually review their ability to achieve their mission and their capability to be efficient and effective in meeting the needs of those they serve. These concerns have generated calls from taxpayers, legislators, advocacy groups, regulators, academicians, and government itself for creating a culture that promotes review, analysis, and improvement.

The use of organizational assessment processes in public sector organizations is not a recent phenomenon. Some government agencies have years of experience in assessment, improvement, and organizational quality practices. The models have evolved over the years, but the interest in understanding operations in order to improve performance is engrained in public service. Accountability is one of the major concepts underlying government service, and those who study public administration have spent a great deal of time trying to determine the best ways to hold public agencies and their leaders accountable (Coe, 2003).

In this atmosphere of continual change, organizational assessment provides a way to examine critical functions and determine the best ways to engage employees in identifying and implementing opportunities for improvement. The ultimate goal is not only to improve efficiency and effectiveness, but to create a culture of assessment, where review, organizational learning, and continuous improvement are part of the everyday business of carrying out the work of government. Introducing and sustaining assessment as part of an organization's culture can provide the critical feedback that enables not only higher levels of performance, but also engages the workforce in a way that utilizes their knowledge and abilities in accomplishing the mission, and improves communication with multiple publics. The responsibility of agency leaders is to introduce, support, and sustain assessment. At its most fundamental, assessment is not just a process. It is a way of thinking about what services are provided, how they are being provided, and how the people who provide them are being supported and enabled to perform the critical functions of government.

There are already a number of successful tools for organizational assessment. Why, then, is it necessary to design assessment processes for the public sector? How is the business of government different from that of the private sector? Government agencies are frequently told that they need to function more like business, and there are some lessons to be learned from the private sector. But, what is also clear is that there are significant and important differences. Government agencies have a legislated set of functions. They often do not have the ability to eliminate programs, even when those programs are ineffective. The mission of government is not grounded in profits and losses, and success in government is not defined by financial measures, as it is in the private sector. There is a different relationship between government agencies and the people for whom they provide services than exists between businesses and their customers. As a result, those who work in government agencies may not be totally comfortable in using assessment tools that focus on the private sector. The best answer may be to take those aspects of existing assessment programs that are common to all organizations, and to customize them to fit the language, the purposes, and the culture of the public sector. The most well-known and successful assessment program, the Baldrige National Quality Program, became a starting point in the process of developing a set of criteria specifically for the public sector.

The process of developing a public sector assessment methodology began as the result of an orientation program being used to introduce the Baldrige process to employees of a government agency in preparation for an assessment. The facilitator, who was a trained Baldrige examiner from outside the organization, noted during the program that people were uncomfortable with some of the concepts. The participants questioned whether, instead, there could be a model that used familiar concepts and terminology and had examples relevant to the work of government. We then realized that having a customized version (what eventually became the Public Sector Assessment and Improvement (PSAI) model) would provide an alternative to having to "translate" the Baldrige criteria for public sector applications, and would allow participants to focus more explicitly on the issues that are most relevant to their own organizational contexts.

The use of structured organizational assessment processes offers public sector organizations an opportunity to examine and improve their operations and create a workplace culture and climate that facilitate excellence. It challenges leaders and employees at all levels to focus on the mission and goals of the agency, and to identify ways of working together—as an organization rather than as individual processes and programs—to provide the best possible services to constituents. Assessment can be a powerful tool for articulating the strengths of the programs and services government provides and for conveying that information to its constituents, as well as for identifying and creating a case for current and future needs, and it does so in a way that capitalizes on a methodology that has been tested and refined in a variety of organizational settings.

## How to Use This Workbook

For all the interest in improving public sector organizations that exists externally, the most meaningful assessments of government can come from government agencies themselves. Many public agencies are, in a very positive and proactive way, actively engaged in assessing and improving their organizational performance. More agencies at the federal, state, and local levels are realizing just how important it is both to evaluate how well they are doing and to convey that information internally to staff, leaders, and decision makers as well as externally to constituents.

This workbook will address:

■ how to determine whether an organizational assessment would benefit a particular organization
■ how to evaluate organizational readiness for assessment, in terms of leadership support, organizational priorities, timing, identification of

cyclical processes, staff engagement, staff time and energy, finances, and relationship to election cycles
- how to select an assessment tool and method that match the available time, financial, and human resources
- how to approach decision makers and identify organizational champions for the process
- how to communicate effectively to internal and external constituents
- how to engage employees in the process

The information in this book is not designed to be proscriptive, nor does it specify "one best way" to proceed. It will not dictate how you should conduct your assessment. Instead, it is intended as a guide to decision making about assessment by creating awareness of the available options and considerations, and by providing a framework for discussions that will lead to determining the right approach for your agency. Each chapter consists of both information and tools, including surveys, exercises, and worksheets that can be used by agencies at all levels to determine whether and how to conduct a meaningful organizational assessment, and how to turn the results of that assessment into organizational improvements. You may choose to use some or all of the worksheets, which can be copied for your use, depending on the choices your agency makes for its assessment process.

For your convenience, the worksheets can be downloaded from

http://www.crcpress.com/product/isbn/9781466579941

# About the Author

**Kathleen Mount Immordino, PhD**, is the director of Organizational Research and Assessment for the Center for Organizational Development and Leadership at Rutgers, The State University of New Jersey (New Brunswick). Prior to joining the Center in 2006, she was a career public sector professional with more than 28 years of experience in state government. Dr. Immordino served as the assistant commissioner for Administration in the New Jersey Department of Transportation, assistant commissioner for Planning and Research in the New Jersey Department of Personnel, and executive director for Planning and Development in the New Jersey Department of Labor, following a number of positions in human resources and strategic planning.

A graduate of Dickinson College (Carlisle, Pennsylvania), Dr. Immordino received an MA from Rider University (Lawrenceville, New Jersey) and a PhD in organizational communication from Rutgers University. She is a past president of the New Jersey chapter of the American Society for Public Administration, and a recipient of the Joseph E. McLean Chapter Service Award. She is a former vice chairperson of the Personnel Subcommittee of the American Society of State Highway and Transportation Officials, and was a member of the publication board for the International Public Management Association for Human Resources. She is a Certified Public Manager and a part-time lecturer in the School of Communication and Information at Rutgers University.

# Chapter 1

# Understanding Organizational Assessment

This chapter introduces the concept of organizational assessment and its value to public sector organizations. It describes the coordinated approach to examining all aspects of the organization, and provides a model for integrating assessment, planning, and improvement. It explains the stages of organizational assessment (information collection, visioning and gap analysis, improvement planning and prioritization, and outcomes and feedback). It discusses the interaction between government organizations and their constituents and why government organizations must develop the ability to assess the expectation levels of constituents.

Tools include:

- Mission Definition Worksheet (Leaders) (#1)
- Operation Source Analysis Worksheet (#2)
- Mission Description Worksheet (All Employees) (#3)

## Organizational Assessment and the Public Sector

What do we mean when we talk about organizational assessment and improvement in public sector organizations?[1] Simply put, assessment and improvement are processes through which a government agency—at the federal, state, or local level—can systematically examine its operation and review its performance to determine current strengths and opportunities for improvement, and then apply the information gained to make positive changes. A commitment to assessment and to the use of assessment processes will provide government agencies with ways to increase organizational performance, maximize resources, and be able to "tell their story;" to communicate with their many and varied constituencies and beneficiaries in a positive way about the good work that is being done. Those who lead, manage, or work in government, as well as those who have an interest in the performance of government, need to understand organizational assessment—what it is, why it's important, how it works, and how it can be applied in a way that addresses the needs of the public sector.

Public sector professionals are very aware that there is no shortage of interest in examining the performance of government. Government agencies are under constant pressure to increase their efficiency, effectiveness, and responsiveness. At the same time, there is pressure for increased transparency and accountability in the way that government conducts its operations. For most of these agencies, the increasing demands for accountability and performance measurement are coming from multiple internal and external sources. The ability of those who work in government to carry out the core functions of their agencies is the subject of review and evaluation from many different groups, including taxpayers, legislators, researchers, and academia. At some levels of government, performance is analyzed on a daily basis in the media: on the Internet, in newspapers, and on television and radio. There are Web sites and blogs devoted to examining government, and it often seems that every agency or program has a dedicated watchdog group or set of critics. While these critiques serve a valuable purpose, often the criteria used do not reflect the things that practitioners know are the most critical, the most fundamental, and the most enduring. The reality is that the overwhelming majority of government agencies do an excellent job of carrying out their mission and balancing needs with available resources. Public sector leaders are well aware, though, that it is often very difficult to convey that message in a way that engenders credibility and support.

In response, government organizations are increasingly adopting organizational assessment and improvement. A systematic approach to assessment provides a way to communicate the high level of work being performed in a way that can be conveyed to the multiple publics served by government, while at the same time acknowledging the opportunities for improvement. The process of assessment recognizes that the ability to effectively accomplish the mission of a government agency's operations depends on not just one but a combination of many factors:

- The organization's leaders
- The staff members and the workforce climate
- The ability to plan
- The use of measurement and information
- The programs and processes that carry out the core functions and the support functions
- The constituents and beneficiaries for whom they provide these services

Because all these factors are important, the ability to make the significant and substantive changes needed to improve organizational performance must be grounded in a comprehensive understanding of the agency, the way in which it functions, and the way these factors interact.

Why is interest in assessment increasing in the public sector? The answer may lie in two words: responsibility and capability. Public sector organizations have an extremely broad scope of responsibility. They provide services for individuals, groups, large and small jurisdictions, and for society at large. They are responsible, in many ways, for the services that enable our society to function. The services provided by government agencies range from public safety and national security to protecting children and the elderly, from managing the criminal justice system to protecting the environment. They impact people's lives every day; the breadth of responsibility is unmatched in any other sector. At the same time, government agencies operate in a maze of paperwork and processes that are designed to ensure equitable treatment, but also can be frustrating to staff and constituents alike and give "government work" a sometimes negative connotation.

Government also must have the capability to carry out these responsibilities. The continual demands for new and different services and service delivery methods, and the requisite costs, are stretching the capability of the public sector to respond. The pressures on public sector employees are complicated by the retirement of the baby boomers who make up a large part of the public sector workforce and the resulting organizational knowledge that leaves with them. Facing decreasing budgets and increasing numbers of people for whom to provide services, government must find ways to increase the capability of their agencies, maximize their available fiscal and human resources, and increase both effectiveness and efficiency.

## Understanding the Demand for Effectiveness and Efficiency

The successful operation of any government agency, regardless of the type or size of the jurisdiction, presents a four-part challenge for public administrators. The challenge at all levels of government is to accomplish the organization's mission by providing high-quality programs and services in a way that:

■ makes the best use of available resources
■ serves the broadest possible population
■ accomplishes the goals of society and of government leaders
■ sustains a workforce that is energized and able to meet these challenges

The ability to fulfill the organization's mission and to meet its goals and objectives is measured in terms of both *effectiveness* and *efficiency*. Although these words are frequently used to discuss organizations, it is important to clearly define both of these terms as they relate to the performance of government.

**Effectiveness** can be defined as the degree to which a government agency consistently meets the perceived need for services at an acceptable level of service quality. It is not always easy to measure, as both parts of the equation can be subjective and dependent on the perspective of the group who is doing the measuring. As Haas (1994) points out, "Being effective is difficult. This is true for people in any complex organization; it is especially true for those in government and public sector jobs, which tend to have overlapping jurisdictions, little autonomy, and multiple constraints."[2] Being effective becomes especially difficult in the face of calls to "do more with less." Part of the problem is that those who are served by government go beyond the traditional definition of "customer." The beneficiaries of government activities include not only the individuals and groups who directly use the services it provides, but also society as a whole. When a municipality provides efficient trash pickup, it is not serving just individual homeowners; the entire town benefits because the sidewalks and roadways are free from trash, enabling them to sustain a community that will attract homeowners, workers, and businesses. Most people will never come in contact with anyone who works for the Centers for Disease Control and Prevention (CDC), but they benefit every day from the research being done there. In many cases, these constituents come to the government because they have no choice of provider. Government is the only source of the services these groups require; for example, those who wish to obtain a driver's license or a Social Security number. In other cases, constituents and beneficiaries are a "captive audience" who have no choice but to participate in certain government processes, such as paying taxes. The public may not have sufficient knowledge to understand the complexity of the processes and training and skills to carry out the tangible benefits that they see.

## CUSTOMERS AND CONSTITUENTS: A LESSON IN SEMANTICS

Much of the literature that has been written about assessment and improvement focuses on the importance of identifying customers and determining their level of satisfaction. Is this applicable in the public sector? There are times when government doesn't act as though it is. While the concept of customers is very recognizable in private sector organizations, it has traditionally not been part of the culture of the public sector. For employees of government agencies, the idea of customers can sometimes be a tough sell, and this can start the conversation about assessment on a difficult note. It may seem like a simple matter of semantics, but it's not uncommon for disputes over terminology to derail efforts toward assessment.

The word customer implies, to many, someone who wants the service or products that an organization provides; people who can choose to select a company's product or engage a service, choose to select the product or service made available by a competitor, or choose not to use that product or service at all. There are two problems with this approach in the public sector. First, many of the services provided in the public sector, such as tax collection, aren't optional. Because people don't have a choice about whether or not to participate in this type of service, it's often difficult for public employees to regard them as customers. Second, it's often difficult to determine who should be considered the actual recipients of the services. When the New Jersey Department of Environmental Protection prepared their initial application for the Governor's Quality Award, they learned that many of their staff members identified the environment as their primary customer, or the endangered species they are mandated to protect. In an assessment conducted in a state Department of Transportation, one engineer named the federal *Manual on Uniform Traffic Control Devices* as his customer, because it was his responsibility to ensure strict adherence to these regulations regardless of the wishes and concerns of contractors, property owners, or citizens.

The word *customer* also has the connotation of a one-to-one relationship where the business is providing something that benefits an individual person. Consider how many motivational posters and books talk about providing excellent service "one customer at a time." There are many examples of individuals who benefit directly from a government-provided service, and many examples of one-to-one transactions in government. A person who receives a Social Security check or unemployment benefits can be described as an individual customer, as can a homeowner whose trash is picked up from the sidewalk in front of his or her house. However, government is more frequently thought of in terms of the broader level of services government agencies provide to everyone in their jurisdictions.

Generally speaking, it is much more productive to encourage people to think in terms of constituents. Constituents are those who benefit from the services provided by government, whether or not they have directly sought those services, either directly through the receipt of a specific service or by reaping the larger societal benefits of government services. Constituents also include those who have an interest in the services provided by government, but in a broader role, such as the legislators who provide funding, or the residents of an adjacent municipality who have an interest in what their neighboring community is doing.

**Efficiency** can be defined as making the best possible use of the resources available in meeting the needs of constituents. Schachter (2007) says that efficiency has been one of the most prominent administrative goals in government for over 25 years, and a key part of every report on government reform in this century. Efficiency takes into account many different types of resources. The typical things that come to mind are time and money, but the resources of government are not limited to funding streams, equipment, and taxpayer dollars. They also include the energy and talent of the staff and the goodwill and trust of the constituents.

Consider the concepts of effectiveness and efficiency in the context of the four challenges of government. If we look at the challenges of government as a model (as shown in Figure 1.1), then effectiveness and efficiency each pertain to one half of the diagram. Effectiveness is related most closely

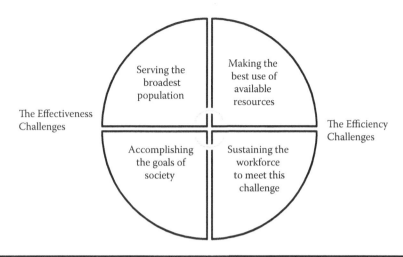

**Figure 1.1   The four challenges of government are represented as parts of a circle, which demonstrates the way that they are interrelated. While all of these challenges contribute to the overall performance of government, those on the left side of the diagram are related to the effectiveness of government performance where those on the right side are related to the efficiency of government.**

o the two challenges on the left side of the diagram—serving the broadest possible population and accomplishing the goals of society. The two challenges on the right side of the diagram, making the best use of available resources and sustaining the workforce needed to carry out these goals, represent efficiency.

Effectiveness and efficiency are without question impacted by the demand for increased government services. One of the considerations for government agencies who are asked to take on responsibilities for new and increasingly diverse services is that, most of the time, the existing range of programs and services also must be maintained. Often, decisions to add services or increase the population served are made without evaluating whether the existing services meet the test of effectiveness and efficiency. Decision makers may not adequately anticipate whether the new responsibilities will change their ability to sustain the effectiveness and efficiency of previously existing services and whether the agency can meet the new expectations. Although efficiency and effectiveness seem to go hand-in-hand, they are not necessarily dependent on each other. It is certainly possible to be effective without being efficient; in fact, this is one of the charges most frequently leveled at various government agencies. It's also possible to be efficient and not effective. While the goal is to achieve both effectiveness and efficiency, they may at times seem to be incompatible concepts or mutually exclusive. Often, government programs and the laws or regulations that implement them contain complex regulatory provisions that all but ensure that these services will never be completely efficient. Initially, it may seem logical to think that it is more important to be effective. The mission of any agency presumes effectiveness. However, efficiency can't be overlooked. Being efficient maximizes the available resources, and can also free up resources, which, in turn, can lead to expanded services and an increased ability to meet goals. It's no wonder that the challenge of evaluating government performance is so difficult.

## What Is Organizational Assessment?

The question becomes how to determine whether a government organization is functioning in a way that is efficient, effective, and capable of addressing the needs of constituents, or from a broader perspective, the needs and requirements of society as a whole. Government agencies, as well as legislators, the public, and various other constituents traditionally measure the effectiveness and efficiency of government programs and services in terms of distinct programs and projects. Many agencies do an excellent job of using data and information to analyze the performance of the programs they monitor or regulate, but may not apply the same level of rigor to examining the internal processes of their own agency. The level of organizational performance required to meet the expectations of these groups requires an integrated approach to organizations, and their systems, programs, and operations. A government agency cannot fully evaluate what it will take to achieve the highest level of effectiveness and efficiency without a systematic examination of the organization and a clear understanding of the entire organization, its people, and its programs.

We often assume that this information is generally available and well-known, but in reality, this type of comprehensive knowledge can be elusive. This understanding must be grounded not just in the perceptions of a few decision makers, but in real, observable, and documented information that clearly outlines, in a structured manner, the current state of the organization. The process through which this evaluation takes place and through which the needed information is obtained and considered is called *organizational assessment*.[3]

The word *assessment* is used frequently in government, and has a number of different meanings depending on the context in which it appears. The description includes:

- The process of apportioning costs, or determining the appropriate level of taxes based on the value and use of property
- A test, interview, or other tool used to evaluate candidates for employment or promotion in a civil service or merit system
- The process of evaluating progress toward learning outcomes, competency development, or skill acquisition in an employee development initiative
- The process of determining the need for training throughout an organization
- Evaluating the accuracy and importance of data, such as intelligence information, or determining the level of risk associated with climate, infrastructure conditions, or pandemic disease

Despite the different meanings, all of these examples of assessment have a shared foundation; each example describes a way of comparing people, practices, or information against agreed upon standards, past performance, perceived need, or known information. When the word *assessment* is used in the context of an organization and its goals, purposes, and performance, making comparisons becomes very important. Comparisons are made as a way to determine and evaluate the current operations and level of effectiveness and efficiency of the organization. Those comparisons might be internal, comparing the organization's performance to that of previous years, or comparing the outcomes of one program or service delivery method against another within the same agency. The comparisons also can be external, such as comparing the organization to others—in the public sector or in other sectors—that perform similar functions. Organizational assessment, in this context, is *a systematic process for examining an organization to create a shared understanding of the current state of those elements that are critical to the successful achievement of its purposes*. Breaking this definition down into its component parts helps identify the key principles of organizational assessment.

**Organizational Assessment** is a systematic process for examining an organization to create a shared understanding of the current state of those elements that are critical to the successful achievement of its purposes.

Assessment is, first and foremost, a ***systematic process***. It provides a structured framework for collecting, combining, and evaluating information that exists throughout the organization. All too often, decisions about the performance and capability of an organization are based on anecdotal information, and the resulting decisions can be very subjective.

Like any other type of performance evaluation, decisions about organizational effectiveness can be heavily influenced by the organization's most recent performance, whether that performance was effective or not. Being systematic means having a structured way of collecting information in which decisions are carefully and conscientiously made about the scope and depth of information that is available, how it is to be obtained, and how it will be used. The word *process*, meaning a sequence of steps and a planned methodology for carrying them out, is also significant. The process of conducting an assessment is in many ways equally as important as the results obtained. It provides a way to involve members of the organization in seeking out needed information and encourages them to use that information to create new knowledge. The process of assessment is action-oriented and extends beyond reporting performance and monitoring the status of the organization. It is the first step in a cycle that begins with assessment and continues to include improvement. It provides a way to stimulate discussion and generate opportunities for improvement, and a methodology for acting on the information obtained. Because it is a systematic process, assessment is:

- consistent
- reliable
- repeatable

This means that the results, or outcomes, can be compared over time.

The assessment process focuses on the ***organization*** as a whole. Introducing and sustaining a program of organizational assessment and improvement in any organization goes beyond examining and improving individual processes or specific work units. Historically, government has been very good at segmenting itself based on the functions and services it provides. It's very common to find that individual programs are monitored and their performance evaluated based on the discrete functions that they use to conduct their operations, rather than on the part they play in larger, organization-wide processes. The example in Figure 1.2 provides a demonstration of how this works. Imagine looking at three divisions who perform different functions in a government agency. Typically, each of the three

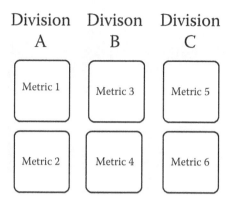

**Figure 1.2 Evaluating programs and services in silos. In this example, each division is focused on collecting data or metrics that deal with specific activities that take place within their unit.**

divisions shown will have developed their own sets of metrics to reflect the performance of their programs or functions. While these metrics may be useful to the individual offices or programs, none of the metrics cross division lines or measure the impact of processes that involve more than one division.

This is often referred to as examining programs in "silos." The result is a collection of metrics that do not reflect the efforts of the whole organization. It's much less common to find organizations that assess themselves across programs and work units and focus on the overall performance of the organization as a working entity. When this broader approach is taken, the result incorporates measures, metrics, and performance into a comprehensive study of the overall management and operation.[4]

Assessment ***creates a shared understanding*** by enabling the members of the organization to collect, review, and compare information so that together they have greater knowledge of the organization than they would have individually. Creating a shared "pool" of information assists them in reaching consensus about the organization. The assessment process brings together the perspectives of people who work in various jobs in different areas and at many different levels. It is often referred to as organizational self-assessment, because the participants in the assessment process are the members of the organization: the employees, managers, and leaders.[5] It involves them in evaluating or diagnosing the organization and recognizes that each person has unique information about what they do, their role in the organization, and how they interact with others. Bringing people together to participate in an assessment is like inviting a group of people to join in putting together a jigsaw puzzle, only in this case, each person owns some of the puzzle pieces. There is no picture on the box for guidance, but everyone believes they know what the finished puzzle should look like. It's very likely that everyone's idea of the finished picture has some elements in common, but differs in many respects based on each person's knowledge and their interpretation of that information. As they negotiate how the puzzle pieces fit together, a picture gradually emerges that all the contributors can see and understand.

Assessment focuses on the **current state** of the organization. It is a forward-looking process that examines where the organization is now and the way that it currently operates, rather than focusing on how it got there. Many traditional forms of performance measurement rely on historical data. While assessment can compare historical and current data to determine trends, the emphasis is on how the operations are currently being performed and how they can be improved.

Assessment identifies the **critical elements** that enable the organization to function. It's a measure of organizational health, grounded in the mission and vision of the organization, and incorporates the structure, leadership, processes, plans, and constituents in the evaluation of overall performance. The process facilitates a review of the organization's priorities, and provides a way to examine whether actions and critical support, including the allocation of financial resources and workforce planning, are aligned with the organization's mission, goals, vision, and plans. Assessment considers major cross-functional issues including strategic planning, human resources, knowledge management, and performance measures that are keys to the success of the organization.

The process of examining government performance involves four progressively more thorough levels of analysis: collecting information, comparing information, analyzing information, and applying information (Figure 1.3).

These levels can be thought of as markers along a continuum, from the most basic processes to the most complex. Most government agencies will fall somewhere within one of these categories. At the primary or first level, information about the performance of the agency, both in terms of processes and outcomes, is collected. This information collection can be the result of internal or external reporting requirements. It is often part of a budget process, and may be used as the basis for reports to inform agency leaders or constituents about progress toward goals. Simply reporting the information

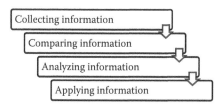

**Figure 1.3   Levels of information usage in government agencies. As government agencies become more sophisticated in using data to evaluate their performance, they "dig deeper" into the information, its meanings, and its uses.**

may be the extent of the agency's intentions; it also can be a first step toward more comprehensive assessment.

At the second level, the information that has been collected is compared to corresponding information so that changes can be identified and tracked. The comparison can be internal and/or external. Internal comparisons can be made to similar performance indicators or results achieved in different time periods, or to levels of performance in other parts of the organization. This same information also can be compared externally, to similar information that exists in other organizations in government or those in different sectors. Comparing information involves indexing the data within a context and using it to determine the current state of performance relative to the results achieved by others. It can be used to identify patterns and to chart and evaluate trends over time.

The third level, analyzing information, requires agencies to interpret the data and consider not only what the information means, but also how it can be applied. At this stage, the agency uses the information not only to examine results and trends, but to analyze their significance. Agencies at this level begin to look at the underlying factors and processes that contribute to how those results are achieved. Leaders and managers must consider not only whether a program is doing well, but whether changes are needed to enable improved performance. Through this type of analysis, agency leaders can consider not only the effectiveness or efficiency of a program or process, but also its utility; that is, whether it is of use to the government agency that provides it in meeting their goals and whether it remains an appropriate use of the funding and other resources available to them.

Finally, the fourth level involves the application of the information in a way that contributes to improving the operations of the program or agency.

## CREATING A SHARED DEFINITION
## OF ORGANIZATIONAL EXCELLENCE

What do we mean when we talk about having or identifying an effective and efficient organization? One of the challenges in undertaking an assessment is to provide a common frame of reference for four key groups: (1) the participants themselves; (2) those people who, while not participants, provide input and contribute information; (3) those who are involved in implementing the resulting improvement opportunities; and (4) those who are simply interested in the process and its results. Using a structured process gives all of these groups a way to talk about the process, regardless of their level of personal involvement. It provides a framework for developing an understanding of organizational improvement for both participants and the nonparticipants who may be curiously observing the assessment process. The assessment process provides a way to operationalize, or define, the concepts of efficiency and effectiveness for all members of the organization using the categories that form the assessment structure and the questions or criteria that are used to examine the organization during the process. It says to leaders, employees, and constituents that being effective in these areas "is the way that efficiency and effectiveness are defined in this organization." Because the assessment process examines several different categories, it also reinforces the idea that organizational excellence is an overall measure of organizational performance, and that effectiveness in one category is not sufficient to create a quality organization. It is the combined effectiveness across all categories that really represents the level of operation for which a participating agency is striving.

## *The Benefits of Assessment*

An assessment process is a structured method of collecting and evaluating cross-functional information about those areas of an agency's operation that are most closely associated with organizational excellence. It is a comprehensive program that begins with understanding the current organization. This information is compared to the vision that leaders have for the organization so that a determination can be made of the gap that exists between the current and the desired way of operating. The knowledge gained during the assessment is used to identify opportunities for improvement and determine the relative priorities of those potential improvements. Finally, project plans are developed and implemented. The feedback from this process forms the starting point for a new cycle of assessment and improvement.

It relies on the participation of those who work in an agency as the "consultants" who collect the information and assess the current state of the organization. Assessment enables participants at all levels to look at the organization and ask if the pieces are in place to create the type of organization it aspires to be. The involvement of employees also provides leaders with an opportunity to build an internal case for change to meet the increasing and evolving demands of their constituencies.

Engaging in this type of process has benefits both for the organization as a whole and for the individuals who have the opportunity to participate. An organizational assessment can:

- provide a structured communication process that takes existing information from across the organization and creates new knowledge through the exchange of information
- define organizational excellence and provide a common understanding of the measures of success
- identify the strengths of the organization
- provide a realistic picture of the challenges and opportunities facing the organization
- help clearly identify both the critical issues and what the relative priorities are for those issues
- create a shared sense of the improvement possibilities

For individual participants, assessment:

- provides a common language for talking about the organization and how it can be improved
- provides a way to engage employees from all areas and at all levels in improving the organization
- focuses the attention of leaders and staff members on the opportunities for improvement
- helps prioritize the challenges facing the agency, thereby providing a "compass" for employees to use in decision making

■ provides a systems approach to thinking about the organization so that people view and understand the impact of their work on the operations of the agency as a whole

A key step in determining the effectiveness of any organization is assessing the clarity of the organization's mission: what you do, for whom you do it, and why. For those considering an organizational assessment, the process begins with a serious discussion about the mission. The worksheet entitled **Defining the Organization's Mission** (page 20) can provide a way to open discussion at the leadership level on the clarity of the mission and the degree to which mission elements are mandated. This worksheet provides a starting point for examining the formal mission as well as any informal missions, and the level to which the agency is obligated to carry out its various functions. It is designed to be completed by organizational leaders at all levels. The responses can be compiled and used as the basis for a group discussion to reach consensus about the mission.

Many organizations have a primary mission and other secondary missions or added functions that have become part of the set of responsibilities over time. Some are required by regulation, law, or statute (Figure 1.4), while others have been adopted as "good ideas."

Government commonly uses the term *mission creep* to describe a type of incremental change in which the mission of the agency is gradually expanded to include functions that were not originally seen as part of the core purpose. If these gradual changes have resulted in a significant difference from where the mission started, people may believe that those changes don't fit the agency's identity even if the leaders believe the new functions

Functions required by state or federal constitution

Functions required by legislation

Functions required by regulation

Functions performed but not required

**Figure 1.4   A good way to begin to analyze an organization's mission is to identify the source of each of the major or core functions.**

are appropriate.[6] These additional functions may or may not be in keeping with the primary mission; some may have outlived their purpose. For this reason, clarification about the responsibilities that should be part of the mission is a valuable starting point. The **Operation Source Analysis Worksheet** (page 21) provides a way for organizational leaders to identify the requirements for the major functions of the agency.

In addition to the leader's perspective on the mission, another important part of preparing to assess the organization and to eventually facilitate organizational change is to get a sense of what employees see as the organization's mission. Many organizations are surprised at the diversity of answers generated, even within very small work units. The assessment process provides a way to get people to think about their perception of the organization's mission, which can spark discussion and potentially change the perceptions of the participants. The organizational and personal learning that takes place during an assessment process may have a significant impact on the individual definitions that people have of the organization's mission.

Why is this important? People who differ in their perception of the organization's core mission also may differ, perhaps significantly, on what the issues and challenges are that face the organization. They may be very sincere and well-meaning in their efforts to do their job, but working at different or cross purposes because they perceive the issues and priorities differently. Reaching consensus on the mission also can help to create consensus on the strengths, the issues, and the challenges that it faces.

One method for gathering this information is through an employee survey (see **Describing the Organization's Mission Worksheet**, page 22). This survey can be distributed either on paper or electronically, using any of the universally available free survey software programs. The language can be customized, for example, to say "division" instead of "agency." Alternatively, it can be used as a discussion script for focus groups. While the questions are fairly straightforward, the responses can be analyzed to determine how convergent (similar) or divergent (different) the responses are. While it is not unusual to see some differences, especially related to job location and job category of the survey takers, generally speaking, employees should have a common idea of the most important overall mission and functions. However, if the range of answers show marked differences, there may not be a shared sense of the organizational mission across the workforce.

For example, the survey asks participants what they believe are the three most important functions of the agency. The purpose of this question is to determine whether there is a shared sense of the core mission and the relative criticality of the operations. As an example, consider these responses from an actual assessment of a physical plant/facilities division. Four answers are listed below in response to the question: "What are the most important functions in this organization?"

1. Maintain/repair physical plant
2. Provide support services: printing and office supplies
3. Future planning for facilities
4. Energy management

These answers seem fairly straightforward, but a closer examination shows differences in how the core mission is perceived. The first two answers identify core maintenance and support functions and the other two identify future-oriented functions: energy management and planning. In this example, the answer might indicate whether the division sees itself as a response and repair operation or as a facilities planning and management unit. In this case, energy management was not identified as a core part of the organization's mission by most employees, although the director of the division believed it was the most important priority. Similarly, an administrative division may want to see whether their employees see their core mission as enforcing rules or providing services to employees. A Call Center manager might want to know whether employees view their job as "answering phones" as opposed to "solving employees' problems."

The second question, which asks how the effectiveness of the organization should be judged, can provide a sense of the criteria that employees believe is being used by agency leaders and by constituents to assess the performance of the organization. This also can be an indicator of what employees believe are the core functions, based on what they believe people outside the organization see as priorities.

# Endnotes

1. The terms *public sector organization* and *government agency* are used interchangeably throughout this book to refer to federal, state, and local governments and to other entities, such as boards, authorities, and commissions. When an example pertains to a particular type of government agency, the language will include a reference to a specific level.

2. Haas, 1994, p. xii.
3. The term *organizational assessment* is used here as a generic term. It includes many types of assessment programs and is not limited to a specific model.
4. While the most useful application of assessment is the analysis of an entire organization, the process also can be applied to subsets, such as divisions, geographically separate offices, or other units. In this case, the assessment process is still conducted within the context of the larger organization. It considers whether the mission and goals of the subunit are consistent with those of the organization as a whole.
5. This book focuses on self-assessment processes, in which the members of the organization are used to conduct the assessment. While assessments can be done by consultants or others external to the organization, the organization loses a valuable opportunity—the benefits that accrue from the organizational and personal learning experienced by the staff and leaders who take part in an assessment process.
6. Organizational identity can be defined as what members of the organization believe to be the definition of its purposes and central characteristics.

# Defining the Organization's Mission

This worksheet is a starting point for our organization to examine our formal and informal missions, and the level to which the organization is obligated to carry out its various functions. You are being asked to complete this worksheet as an organizational leader. Please give candid and complete answers to the questions, so that the responses can be used to help us reach consensus on the mission.

## 1. Which of the following best applies to this organization?

○ We have a formal, documented mission statement

○ We do not have a formal mission statement, but the mission is clear to leaders and staff

○ We have multiple missions and the priority is not clear

○ There is little agreement on a specific mission for our organization

## 2. Please enter the text of the mission statement if it exists; if there is no formal mission statement, please enter what you believe to be the mission and/or the components of the mission.

## 3. Do you believe the mission is clear to staff members at all levels?

○ Clear to employees at all levels

○ Clear to employees at most, but not all levels

○ Clear to employees at some, but not all levels

○ Not clear to employees

## 4. Does the organization have a vision statement?

○ Yes, there is a formal vision statement

○ There is no formal vision statement, but the vision for the organization has been discussed and is clear to leaders

○ There is no formal vision statement, but the vision for the organization has been discussed and communicated to all staff members

○ The vision for the organization has not been formally discussed

**Worksheet #1**

# Operation Source Analysis

This Worksheet provides a way for identifying the major functions of the organization, agency or program and the source of function. Identifying the initiating legislation, regulation, or requirement can help examine how these functions relate to the mission of the organization.

**1. In the boxes that follow, list up to 10 major functions performed in your area of operation and identify. Select the category that best describes the source through which it is required. For example, if you indicate that the source of a function is the state constitution, that means that it is required by the state constitution, not that it is allowable or permitted by the state constitution.**

| | U.S. Constitution | State Constitution | Federal legislation | State legislation | Local legislation | Federal regulation | State regulation | Local regulation | Not formally required |
|---|---|---|---|---|---|---|---|---|---|
| 1. | ○ | ○ | ○ | ○ | ○ | ○ | ○ | ○ | ○ |
| 2. | ○ | ○ | ○ | ○ | ○ | ○ | ○ | ○ | ○ |
| 3. | ○ | ○ | ○ | ○ | ○ | ○ | ○ | ○ | ○ |
| 4. | ○ | ○ | ○ | ○ | ○ | ○ | ○ | ○ | ○ |
| 5. | ○ | ○ | ○ | ○ | ○ | ○ | ○ | ○ | ○ |
| 6. | ○ | ○ | ○ | ○ | ○ | ○ | ○ | ○ | ○ |
| 7. | ○ | ○ | ○ | ○ | ○ | ○ | ○ | ○ | ○ |
| 8. | ○ | ○ | ○ | ○ | ○ | ○ | ○ | ○ | ○ |
| 9. | ○ | ○ | ○ | ○ | ○ | ○ | ○ | ○ | ○ |
| 10. | ○ | ○ | ○ | ○ | ○ | ○ | ○ | ○ | ○ |

Worksheet #2

# Describing the Organization's Mission

The purpose of this worksheet is to collect information that will help our agency clarify the organization's mission and the most important measures of our agency's success. As you complete this survey, please think about the agency as a whole, not just the section or program in which you work. Please complete this worksheet based on what you believe to be true based on your experiences, not the stated or public positions of your agency or its leaders.

1. What do you believe are the five most important functions of this agency?

1. _____

2. _____

3. _____

4. _____

5. _____

2. What are the five things this organization does best?

1. _____

2. _____

3. _____

4. _____

5. _____

3. What are the top three factors you believe the leaders of this organization use to evaluate its effectiveness?

1. _____

2. _____

3. _____

4. What are the top three factors you believe people outside the organization use to measure its effectiveness?

1. _____

2. _____

3. _____

5. What are the top three factors you believe should be used to measure the organization's effectiveness?

1. _____

2. _____

3. _____

**Worksheet #3**

# Chapter 2

# Determining Readiness for Assessment

This chapter begins with an overview of the planning process and an examination of the factors that must be considered before a public sector organization should undertake an organizational assessment, including the level of leadership support, timing and agency priorities, and workforce climate. It considers how these factors apply to a specific organization, and how they should be presented and considered in the decision making process.

Tools include:

- Assessment Goal Setting Worksheet (#4)
- Peak Time and Availability Worksheet (#5)
- Organizational Climate Assessment Worksheet (#6)
- Identifying Constituents Worksheet (#7)
- Constituent Expectation Worksheet (#8)
- Assessment Readiness Checklist (#9)

An organizational assessment is an excellent starting point for any public sector agency looking to evaluate and improve the way in which it functions. It makes the employees of an agency the lead researchers in developing and documenting information and in recommending options for future direction. The shared knowledge produced by the assessment can have a very powerful effect on the way people perceive things by making them aware of strengths and opportunities for improvement previously unknown to them. While this is a strong incentive for proceeding, it is important to remember that the process requires an investment of time, energy, and resources. The purpose of this preplanning stage is to determine whether the time and resources that must be invested in the process are available and to decide whether the agency is willing to commit them. Government agencies should approach the decision to implement an assessment the same way that they would any other major project. This means doing a careful job of identifying the steps to be taken and the key decisions to be made.

## Consider the Source

The suggestion to undertake an organizational assessment can originate from any number of sources, both internal and external to the agency (Figure 2.1). It can come from the top down, from a newly appointed organizational leader seeking a way to learn about its level of effectiveness or efficiency, or from an existing leader, manager, or program director who wants to enhance the quality of programs and services. The idea can "bubble up," in other words, being generated from within any administrative or technical/program area. External forces, including constituents, beneficiaries, advocacy, or regulatory groups, also can initiate an assessment process as a way to address their concerns over program quality or service delivery.

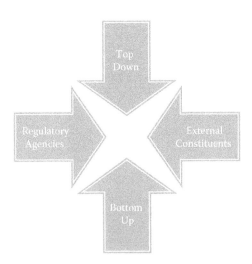

**Figure 2.1** **The interest in organizational assessment can come from any direction. Which of these arrows represents the initiator(s) for your agency?**

It's also important to understand the reasons behind the interest in organizational assessment. Regardless of where the idea originates, leaders must be clear about the reason why an assessment is being proposed and be willing to share that reasoning throughout the agency. Although it might seem obvious (to evaluate the current performance of the agency), there can be many different perspectives among different staff and constituent groups on why an assessment is needed and what an assessment can accomplish. These perspectives can translate into different expectations. The motivation for initiating an assessment process can be proactive, such as looking to improve the organization or to achieve recognition for outstanding programs and services, or reactive, for example, recognizing that there has been a crisis in agency performance, and using the assessment to plan a response. Some other possible reasons for undertaking this type of process can include:

■ To set the stage for a strategic planning initiative
■ To provide new leaders with an understanding of the agency
■ To improve communication across and among the agency's leaders and major work areas
■ In response to an identified problem
■ To determine the best possible use of an infusion of resources
■ To determine how to reallocate reduced resources

It is important that everyone involved start with a clear understanding of the goals for the assessment and a clear sense of what the agency hopes to achieve. Leaders also must consider whether they are willing to learn about the good news and the bad news—both the strengths and the obstacles that face them. **The Assessment Goal Setting Worksheet** (page 35) provides a focal point for discussions about the assessment, the goals of the assessment process, and the intended use of the assessment outcomes. Organizational leaders can complete this chart to identify the importance of each of the reasons/goals. The responses can be compared and used to initiate a discussion at the senior staff level, or highest management level if the assessment is being done for a division, unit, or other subsection of an agency, to clarify and reach consensus on the goals. Similarly, it is important that leaders have a shared expectation of the likely outcomes and some agreement on what they hope to achieve. Just because the process has been described to them does not mean that they will agree on how the process will take place and how focused the assessment leaders should be on the process outcomes. For example, a leader may feel strongly that the only purpose for the assessment is to identify strengths and priorities for improvement, and that the assessment participants should not be part of the process to create agreement on functions, goals, or relative priorities. Reaching consensus on the intended outcomes will help shape the process itself, and the way expectations are communicated to participants and observers.

This information also can be used later to provide information to agency employees about the rationale for conducting the assessment.

## BEST PRACTICES

Find a champion: Try to identify at least one high-level leadership person who will support the process—vocally and when possible, visibly—by attending briefings, sending encouraging notes, or addressing team members.

## Determining Readiness for Assessment

Having the political will or a clearly defined purpose prior to undertaking an assessment does not guarantee that the organization is actually ready to do so. Before beginning the process, those involved in planning the assessment must evaluate whether the agency is ready to engage in an assessment process. Berman and Wang (2000) studied the need for government organizations implementing performance measurement systems to first ensure that they had the capacity, which includes having management support, along with the ability to collect information, analyze the resulting data and apply the information to operations. The same need is true to determine capacity and ability in designing and implementing assessment processes. Determining organizational readiness for an assessment requires, at a minimum, that the agency evaluates each of the following factors:

◼ The level of leadership support
◼ Timing and agency priorities

- The current workforce climate
- Constituent relations

This information can be developed through discussions or focus groups, or by using a series of questions related to each of these factors. The **Assessment Readiness Checklist Worksheet** (page 43) is a tool that can be used to gain some basic insight in these areas, and allows the planners to evaluate how much agreement there is on the answers.

## Leadership Support

The support of the agency head—whether it is a commissioner or secretary in federal or state government, or a mayor, city manager, or township administrator in local government—can be invaluable in implementing an assessment process. The same is true for the support of the senior leadership team of the agency. Whether or not the senior leaders are the ones who initiate the process, their support opens many internal and external doors. Their open or implied endorsement provides a go-ahead signal to the agency as a whole that encourages participation and enables access to information that exists in all parts and all levels of the organization. It also can serve an important purpose by providing access to various external constituent groups and sending a formal signal that their participation is both requested and welcomed. The support of agency leaders often provides a bridge to the political leaders associated with the jurisdiction. Leadership support indicates willingness to make the organization's resources available. It can foster a comfort level throughout the organization by sanctioning the process through communication with employees and constituents. The need for leadership support extends throughout the assessment process and beyond, as the assessment outcomes are put to use (Figure 2.2).

One of the most important areas of concern for participants and staff in general is the level of commitment the agency leaders make to the project planning and improvement phase and to the implementation of the identified improvement projects (Figure 2.3). Prior to any implementation decision, it is important to determine whether senior leaders are committed not just to undertaking an assessment process, but also to implementing at least some of the recommendations for improvements that develop from the process. There is nothing more frustrating in an assessment process than for employees to invest their time and energy in producing an analysis and recommendations,

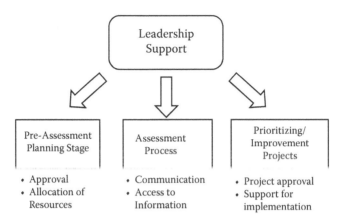

**Figure 2.2   Leadership support is essential through every stage of the assessment process.**

| *Consider the Following Questions:* |
| --- |
| • Are senior leaders interested in determining the current level of performance? |
| • Are senior leaders willing to support an assessment process? |
| • Are senior leaders willing to make the results of the process available throughout the organization? |
| • Are senior leaders willing to act on the results of the process and implement improvement recommendations? |

**Figure 2.3   Leadership support considerations.**

only to realize that the action plans will not be enacted. In addition to being counterproductive, it makes it much less likely that employee participation will take place willingly during any future assessment efforts.

## Timing and Agency Priorities

A second factor to consider in planning an assessment process is timing, particularly as it relates to other priorities in the organization (Figure 2.4). In other words, what else may be going on in the organization that will compete for the available resources at the point in time when the assessment would take place? Will the staff and leadership be able to devote both attention and resources to the process?

| Consider the Following Questions: |
|---|
| • Are there any major events or agency comittments that would prohibit an assessment at this time? |
| • Are resources currently available, including the time and energy of staff, to allow an assessment to take place? |

**Figure 2.4    Timing and agency priorities.**

Just as there is no "best" time to undertake many types of projects, there is no one best time to schedule an assessment. It depends on the core processes and the demands on a particular agency and must balance the need for assessment against the available resources. There are certain times during the annual cycle when the work of the agency makes it predictable that the needed level of attention would not be available. During those time frames, it would be less advantageous to schedule an assessment. Consider these examples:

∎ An oceanfront community with publicly maintained beaches relies heavily on tourism as a funding source. They would be less likely to succeed if they schedule an assessment during the summer season when the attention of the staff must be focused on tourism as a critical function. The likelihood of success would be much higher if they would instead use the winter as a time when staff would be more available and have more "down time."

∎ An agency considering conducting an assessment wants to include their financial staff as participants in the process, since management believes that this unit is one of several that should be a "priority" to be looked at in the assessment. The time period being considered for the assessment is the same block of time that is, each year, devoted to preparation of the annual budget. It would be advantageous to schedule the assessment for a time after completion of the budget process.

The **Peak Time and Availability Worksheet** (page 36) can be used to identify the peak workload or mission critical time frames for each of the major organizational components that might take part in an organizational assessment. While it does not address every situation or unanticipated crisis, it provides a general guideline—much like online scheduling software—to indicate the most ideal (or least problematic) time for the participation phase of an assessment process. It also can be used to determine the availability of individual employee groups (by function, title, or location) and provides a picture that can be useful in determining if an assessment should be divided and conducted during different time periods for different parts of the organization.

## *The Election Cycle*

Another event that can impact the timing of an assessment is the election cycle. Because there is a probability that the organization is going to have new leadership as a result of an election, it's generally counterproductive to be in the middle of an assessment process during a change of an administration. Take into account not only a change in elected officials, but changes in appointed officials even if there is no change in party. There are two options for timing. The first is to schedule the assessment process in such a way that the current administration has the ability to support the process and enact at least some of its recommendations. The second is to complete an assessment immediately prior to the arrival of a new administration. The information from an assessment could potentially be very helpful in the transition from one administration to the next, for their use in learning the organization and setting priorities. However, the potential usefulness should be balanced against the possibility that the organization is investing time and energy and the information may not be welcomed or used.

The most important thing in scheduling an assessment is to carefully consider the timing and make a conscious decision based on the best possible time frame.

# The Internal View: Workforce Climate

As critical as leadership support can be, the support and engagement of the agency's workforce can be just as significant to the outcome of the assessment and improvement effort. Those planning the implementation must consider what the potential response of the agency's workforce might be. Therefore, a third consideration in planning is to determine the prevailing workforce climate, which can have either a positive or negative impact on the response of the staff (both participants and nonparticipants) to

| Consider the Following Questions: |
|---|
| • Are staff members willing to contribute time and energy to the process? |
| • Are staff members willing to contribute information? |
| • Does the organizational climate suggest that staff members would be candid about the organization? |
| • Would it be difficult to get volunteer employee participants? |
| • Are managers willing to allow their staff to participate? |

**Figure 2.5   Workforce climate considerations.**

an assessment process. Workforce climate can represent several different dimensions, including:

■ Openness to change
■ Willingness to participate
■ Support for the open exchange of information

The success of the initiative relies in large part on the willingness of the staff to participate by providing the information needed, serving as active participants in the process, and accepting and implementing the outcomes (Figure 2.5).

If the organizational climate is negative, it may be difficult to encourage people to participate in the assessment process or, at the least, to provide the needed information about their particular area of responsibility.[1] A positive workforce climate suggests that people would be more willing to participate. Their willingness to participate also can be affected by the degree to which they believe that management is committed to the process and willing to listen to the outcomes.

The **Organizational Climate Assessment[2] Worksheet** (page 38) can be used to gain a sense of the current organizational climate.

# The External View: Constituent Relations

So far, we have considered how assessment can benefit the organization itself and its employees, but also it is important at the beginning of any discussion about assessment to consider external parties. Public sector organizations have a unique opportunity to impact the lives of those for whom they provide programs and services. At all levels, including federal, state, and local government, as well as commissions, boards, authorities, and other agencies whose mission is to serve the public, the key question is how best to meet the needs of those constituents. Government agencies constantly interact with their constituents, and the expectations of those groups for both the type and the scope of services an agency provides change on a regular basis. This creates an ongoing demand not only for new and different services, some of which are needed for new or expanding constituent groups, but also for innovation in the way existing services are provided.

The introduction of assessment processes in government is in many ways a response to demands that agencies become proactive in examining and improving their ability to function. Public sector organizations that do not have a process in place to evaluate their operation and improve their efficiency and effectiveness are likely to find that the measures of their success are being defined and imposed by individuals and constituent groups outside the organization. In many cases, the opinions of these groups about what constitutes effective performance, what should be measured, and how, could differ greatly from that of those working within the organization.

In 2008, an Association of Government Accountants (AGA) survey showed that there is an "expectation gap" between what citizens believe they should know about federal, state, and local government and the information that is available to them. Citizens reported a distrust of government at all levels based not only on what information is or is not provided, but also on the perceived lack of openness and the attitude of government toward making this information available in user friendly ways.

The very public nature of these concerns has created what is often referred to as a crisis in public confidence. Thinking about the well-known adage that "perception is reality," the public may well believe that there is no good news to be had when it comes to talking about government performance. This "crisis" perspective often fails to recognize what those who work in the public sector know to be true: that there are an overwhelming number of positive performance outcomes generated by government and that government itself is leading the charge toward improved organizational effectiveness. Government agencies are often the strongest advocates for undertaking assessment and improvement initiatives.

It is also important to remember that public sector organizations have internal as well as external constituents. Many of the administrative functions, including human resources, information technology, facilities, mail processing, and motor pools, generally do not deal with the public in any substantive way, but that doesn't mean that they don't have constituents. Instead, they are responsible for a set of internal customers who also have expectations for the level of service they receive.

Many people can identify their primary constituents, generally the group for whom they provide their highest profile service, but do not always consider the variety of groups and individuals who rely on them or who control their access to resources. The **Identifying Constituents Worksheet** (page 41) can be used as a brainstorming tool to identify internal and external constituents prior to undertaking an organizational assessment.[3]

Knowing who your constituents are is an important consideration and provides a reference point when considering programs, services, and the way that staff members interact with constituents. It also is important to understand the measures of organizational success that those constituents apply when thinking about a government agency. Once a list of constituents has been generated, the **Constituent Expectations Worksheet** (page 42) can be used to identify the measures that the various constituents employ.

## Evaluating Organizational Readiness

There are many facets of organizational readiness. The **Assessment Readiness Checklist Worksheet** (page 43) summarizes the many issues that have been covered in this chapter. The worksheet serves as a checklist of considerations by incorporating all the readiness areas into one list. However, the information collected using this worksheet will not provide a definitive answer to the question of whether your organization is ready to proceed with an assessment, how you should conduct it, or when would be the best time. It, however, will provide insight into the likelihood that your organization would benefit from an assessment, and may indicate areas of concern in whether to proceed with an assessment for a particular agency or program at a particular point in time.

**BEST PRACTICES: GET PEOPLE TO BELIEVE IN THE CONCEPT AND PROCESS, NOT THE LABEL OR NAME**

In the early stages of introducing an assessment process, people will sometimes focus on the name or label that they believe goes with it. They may express skepticism, saying, "We've already done quality, we've been through total quality management" or "we've done strategic planning." Communicate to participants and nonparticipants that this is not the newest flavor of the month, but a concept that focuses on collecting information and making fact-based determinations. It's built around concepts that have been identified repeatedly as being critical to organizational effectiveness, and this simply provides a systematic approach to applying them. The focus should be on mutual agreement to study and improve the organization, not on a label.

# Endnotes

1. The information developed during an assessment can be used to try to correct or rebalance a negative organizational climate, although this is not a primary outcome.
2. This worksheet is an adaptation of the Organizational Climate Assessment developed by the Center for Organizational Development and Leadership, Rutgers University, and is used with the permission of the author and NACUBO.
3. This exercise is particularly useful in a workshop where participants list as many constituents as possible, then work in small groups to compare results. Encouraging discussion tends to generate additional responses and leads to a much fuller final list.

# Assessment Goal Setting

Since the success of an organizational assessment can depend on having clear and agreed upon goals, it is important to get a sense from the leadership of this organization about the reasons for undertaking this process. For each of the following statements, please indicate whether you see it as one of your goals in implementing as assessment process.

## 1. What are your goals in considering an organizational assessment process?

|  | Primary goal | Secondary goal | Minor/not a goal |
|---|---|---|---|
| Being proactive | O | O | O |
| To apply for/achieve an award or quality designation | O | O | O |
| To set the stage for a strategic planning initiative | O | O | O |
| To provide new leaders with an understanding of the agency | O | O | O |
| To improve communication across and among the agency's leaders | O | O | O |
| To improve communication across and among major work areas | O | O | O |
| To address an identified problem | O | O | O |
| To determine the best use of an infusion of resources | O | O | O |
| To determine how to allocate reduced resources | O | O | O |
| To respond to increasing demand for services | O | O | O |
| To respond to changes in available talent | O | O | O |
| As a way to deal with changing and conflicting priorities | O | O | O |

## 2. How important to you are each of these assessment process outcomes?

|  | Most important | Very important | Important | Less important | Not important |
|---|---|---|---|---|---|
| Identify organizational strengths | O | O | O | O | O |
| Identify opportunities for improvement | O | O | O | O | O |
| Create agreement on core and support functions | O | O | O | O | O |
| Create a shared understanding of constituents and beneficiaries | O | O | O | O | O |
| Create agreement on key goals | O | O | O | O | O |
| Create agreement on critical issues | O | O | O | O | O |
| Determine the relative priority of improvement opportunities | O | O | O | O | O |
| Increase shared knowledge about the agency | O | O | O | O | O |
| Build a shared sense of responsibility for organizational outcomes | O | O | O | O | O |

Worksheet #4

# Peak Time and Availability

Identify each organizational component (division, office, workgroup, or employee group) in the agency which is being considered for participation in an assessment. Use this as a planning tool to determine, first, whether that organizational component is critical for participation in the assessment by placing each component into a numbered group (on a scale of 1–5, with 5 meaning that they are critical to the planned assessment). Then, within each group, identify their peak workload/mission critical time frames. This can form the basis of a discus sion about how and when to schedule the assessment process.

## 1. CATEGORY 5: Most critical
List the units considered most critical for participation in the planned assessment. For each unit, indicate the peak workload times for each using the months of the year.

|    | J | F | M | A | M | J | J | A | S | O | N | D |
|----|---|---|---|---|---|---|---|---|---|---|---|---|
| 1. | ☐ | ☐ | ☐ | ☐ | ☐ | ☐ | ☐ | ☐ | ☐ | ☐ | ☐ | ☐ |
| 2. | ☐ | ☐ | ☐ | ☐ | ☐ | ☐ | ☐ | ☐ | ☐ | ☐ | ☐ | ☐ |
| 3. | ☐ | ☐ | ☐ | ☐ | ☐ | ☐ | ☐ | ☐ | ☐ | ☐ | ☐ | ☐ |
| 4. | ☐ | ☐ | ☐ | ☐ | ☐ | ☐ | ☐ | ☐ | ☐ | ☐ | ☐ | ☐ |
| 5. | ☐ | ☐ | ☐ | ☐ | ☐ | ☐ | ☐ | ☐ | ☐ | ☐ | ☐ | ☐ |

## 2. CATEGORY 4
List the units considered next most critical for participation in the planned assessment. For each unit, indicate the peak workload times for each using the months of the year.

|    | J | F | M | A | M | J | J | A | S | O | N | D |
|----|---|---|---|---|---|---|---|---|---|---|---|---|
| 1. | ☐ | ☐ | ☐ | ☐ | ☐ | ☐ | ☐ | ☐ | ☐ | ☐ | ☐ | ☐ |
| 2. | ☐ | ☐ | ☐ | ☐ | ☐ | ☐ | ☐ | ☐ | ☐ | ☐ | ☐ | ☐ |
| 3. | ☐ | ☐ | ☐ | ☐ | ☐ | ☐ | ☐ | ☐ | ☐ | ☐ | ☐ | ☐ |
| 4. | ☐ | ☐ | ☐ | ☐ | ☐ | ☐ | ☐ | ☐ | ☐ | ☐ | ☐ | ☐ |
| 5. | ☐ | ☐ | ☐ | ☐ | ☐ | ☐ | ☐ | ☐ | ☐ | ☐ | ☐ | ☐ |

## 3. CATEGORY 3
List the units considered the next most critical for participation in the planned assessment. For each unit, indicate the peak workload times for each using the months of the year.

|    | J | F | M | A | M | J | J | A | S | O | N | D |
|----|---|---|---|---|---|---|---|---|---|---|---|---|
| 1. | ☐ | ☐ | ☐ | ☐ | ☐ | ☐ | ☐ | ☐ | ☐ | ☐ | ☐ | ☐ |
| 2. | ☐ | ☐ | ☐ | ☐ | ☐ | ☐ | ☐ | ☐ | ☐ | ☐ | ☐ | ☐ |
| 3. | ☐ | ☐ | ☐ | ☐ | ☐ | ☐ | ☐ | ☐ | ☐ | ☐ | ☐ | ☐ |
| 4. | ☐ | ☐ | ☐ | ☐ | ☐ | ☐ | ☐ | ☐ | ☐ | ☐ | ☐ | ☐ |
| 5. | ☐ | ☐ | ☐ | ☐ | ☐ | ☐ | ☐ | ☐ | ☐ | ☐ | ☐ | ☐ |

Worksheet #5

# Peak Time and Availability

## 4. CATEGORY 2

List the units considered the next most critical for participation in the planned assessment. For each unit, indicate the peak workload times for each using the months of the year.

|    | J | F | M | A | M | J | J | A | S | O | N | D |
|----|---|---|---|---|---|---|---|---|---|---|---|---|
| 1. | ☐ | ☐ | ☐ | ☐ | ☐ | ☐ | ☐ | ☐ | ☐ | ☐ | ☐ | ☐ |
| 2. | ☐ | ☐ | ☐ | ☐ | ☐ | ☐ | ☐ | ☐ | ☐ | ☐ | ☐ | ☐ |
| 3. | ☐ | ☐ | ☐ | ☐ | ☐ | ☐ | ☐ | ☐ | ☐ | ☐ | ☐ | ☐ |
| 4. | ☐ | ☐ | ☐ | ☐ | ☐ | ☐ | ☐ | ☐ | ☐ | ☐ | ☐ | ☐ |
| 5. | ☐ | ☐ | ☐ | ☐ | ☐ | ☐ | ☐ | ☐ | ☐ | ☐ | ☐ | ☐ |

## 5. CATEGORY 1: Least critical

List the units considered the least critical for participation in the planned assessment. For each unit, indicate the peak workload times for each using the months of the year.

|    | J | F | M | A | M | J | J | A | S | O | N | D |
|----|---|---|---|---|---|---|---|---|---|---|---|---|
| 1. | ☐ | ☐ | ☐ | ☐ | ☐ | ☐ | ☐ | ☐ | ☐ | ☐ | ☐ | ☐ |
| 2. | ☐ | ☐ | ☐ | ☐ | ☐ | ☐ | ☐ | ☐ | ☐ | ☐ | ☐ | ☐ |
| 3. | ☐ | ☐ | ☐ | ☐ | ☐ | ☐ | ☐ | ☐ | ☐ | ☐ | ☐ | ☐ |
| 4. | ☐ | ☐ | ☐ | ☐ | ☐ | ☐ | ☐ | ☐ | ☐ | ☐ | ☐ | ☐ |
| 5. | ☐ | ☐ | ☐ | ☐ | ☐ | ☐ | ☐ | ☐ | ☐ | ☐ | ☐ | ☐ |

(Continued) Worksheet #5

# Organizational Climate Assessment

Organizational Climate Assessment

Adapted from the Organizational Climate Assessment designed by the Center for Organzational Development and Leadership at Rutgers, The State University of New Jersey.

## 1. The Organization

| | Strongly disagree | Disagree | Agree | Strongly agree |
|---|---|---|---|---|
| I am proud to be part of this organization | O | O | O | O |
| I would recommend this organization as a good place to work | O | O | O | O |
| People from different areas work cooperatively to achieve a common goal | O | O | O | O |

## 2. My Department: Collaboration and Communication

| | Strongly disagree | Disagree | Agree | Strongly agree |
|---|---|---|---|---|
| Communication between people works well | O | O | O | O |
| People help each other out and work as a team | O | O | O | O |
| Sincere efforts are made to obtain the opinions and thoughts of people who work here | O | O | O | O |
| Employees are encouraged to provide feedback | O | O | O | O |
| Collaboration is good between leaders and staff members | O | O | O | O |
| Teamwork is valued | O | O | O | O |
| Leaders and staff members agree on what constitutes good work | O | O | O | O |
| Employees are aware of projects and plans for the department | O | O | O | O |
| People trust one another | O | O | O | O |
| People treat each other with dignity and respect | O | O | O | O |
| People actively seek the participation of others who represent different backgrounds and points of view | O | O | O | O |

**Worksheet #6**

# Organizational Climate Assessment

## 3. My Department Leadership

| | Strongly disagree | Disagree | Agree | Strongly agree |
|---|:---:|:---:|:---:|:---:|
| Leaders are visible to me on a regular basis | ○ | ○ | ○ | ○ |
| Leaders are accessible | ○ | ○ | ○ | ○ |
| I clearly understand the department's mission and goals | ○ | ○ | ○ | ○ |
| Leaders value my suggestions | ○ | ○ | ○ | ○ |
| Policies are administered in a fair and consistent manner | ○ | ○ | ○ | ○ |
| There is a clear sense of direction | ○ | ○ | ○ | ○ |
| Our leaders embrace a philosophy of service and assessment | ○ | ○ | ○ | ○ |

## 4. My Department: Supervision

| | Strongly Disagree | Disagree | Agree | Strongly Agree |
|---|:---:|:---:|:---:|:---:|
| Supervisors practice open communication | ○ | ○ | ○ | ○ |
| Supervisors are open to feedback | ○ | ○ | ○ | ○ |
| Supervisors provide useful feedback on job performance | ○ | ○ | ○ | ○ |
| Supervisors act in fair and ethical ways | ○ | ○ | ○ | ○ |
| Supervisors understand what is required to do my job | ○ | ○ | ○ | ○ |

(Continued) **Worksheet #6**

# Organizational Climate Assessment

## 5. My Department: Work and Opportunity

| | Strongly Disagree | Disagree | Agree | Strongly Agree |
|---|---|---|---|---|
| I know the areas for which I am responsible | ○ | ○ | ○ | ○ |
| I like the work I do | ○ | ○ | ○ | ○ |
| My job gives me a feeling of personal accomplishment | | | | |
| My present assignment allows me to fully use my skills and abilities | ○ | ○ | ○ | ○ |
| My job is challenging | ○ | ○ | ○ | ○ |
| The amount of work I am expected to do is reasonable | ○ | ○ | ○ | ○ |
| I have an opportunity to develop new skills | ○ | ○ | ○ | ○ |
| I feel good about the security of my present job | ○ | ○ | ○ | ○ |
| I receive the necessary training and professional development to be successful | ○ | ○ | ○ | ○ |
| I would recommend my department as a good place to work | ○ | ○ | ○ | ○ |
| I am satisfied with my physical working conditions | ○ | ○ | ○ | ○ |
| I have enough information to do my job efficiently and effectively | ○ | ○ | ○ | ○ |
| In comparison with people in similar jobs in this organization, I feel my pay is fair | ○ | ○ | ○ | ○ |
| My potential is being recognized | ○ | ○ | ○ | ○ |
| My coworkers perform up to my expectations | ○ | ○ | ○ | ○ |
| I am satisfied with the recognition I receive for doing a good job | ○ | ○ | ○ | ○ |

## 6. Overall, how would you rate this agency as a place to work?

| Poor | Fair | Acceptable | Good | Outstanding |
|---|---|---|---|---|
| ○ | ○ | ○ | ○ | ○ |

**(Continued) Worksheet #6**

# Identifying Constituents

Complete the Constituent worksheet individually. Identify your constituents – those for whom your agency provides services – and list them in the appropriate category. Keep in mind that constituents can be internal or external to the organization. Form small groups and compare responses. Each group will select a spokesperson to report out so that a master chart can be developed.

| Individuals | Groups and Organizations | Professional Associations | Legislative and governmental bodies | Regulatory agencies |
|---|---|---|---|---|
|  |  |  |  |  |
|  |  |  |  |  |
|  |  |  |  |  |
|  |  |  |  |  |
|  |  |  |  |  |
|  |  |  |  |  |
|  |  |  |  |  |
|  |  |  |  |  |
|  |  |  |  |  |

# Constituent Expectation Worksheet

**Enter each constituent identified in the Constituent Identification worksheet in the Constituent Group column. Identify what type of constituent it is, using the headings from Worksheet 7 (I = individual, G = groups and organizations, P = professional associations, L = legislative and governmental bodies, R = regulatory agencies). For each constituent group, identify one or more ways this constituent measures your success. For example, the matrix for a transportation agency may begin with examples such as these:**

| Constituent group | Type (I,G,P,L,R) | Measure |
|---|---|---|
| Federal Highway Administration | L | Accidents per lane mile |
| Drivers | I | Travel time |
| State legislators | G | Dollars spent per lane mile |

| Constituent Worksheet<br>How does each of these groups measure your success? | | |
|---|---|---|
| Constituent Group | Type (I,G,P,L,R) | Measure |
| | | |
| | | |
| | | |
| | | |
| | | |
| | | |
| | | |
| | | |
| | | |
| | | |
| | | |

Worksheet #8

# Assessment Readiness Checklist

This checklist is designed to help evaluate whether an organization is ready to engage in an organizational self-assessment process at this time. You may be asked to consider your part of the agency, or the organization as a whole when answering these questions. For each item, please indicate how strongly you agree or disagree with the statement.

## 1. Leadership

| | Strongly agree | Agree | Disagree | Strongly disagree |
|---|---|---|---|---|
| Senior leaders are interested in determining the current level of performance | O | O | O | O |
| Senior leaders are willing to support an assessment process | O | O | O | O |
| Senior leaders are open to receiving feedback about the organization | O | O | O | O |
| Senior leaders are willing to make the results of the process available throughout the organization | O | O | O | O |
| Senior leaders are willing to act on the results of the process and implement improvement recommendations | O | O | O | O |

## 2. Timing

| | Strongly agree | Agree | Disagree | Strongly disagree |
|---|---|---|---|---|
| There are no major events or agency commitments which would prohibit an assessment at this time | O | O | O | O |
| Resources are currently available, including the time and energy of staff members, to allow an assessment to take place | O | O | O | O |

## 3. Workforce Climate

| | Strongly agree | Agree | Disagree | Strongly disagree |
|---|---|---|---|---|
| Staff members are willing to contribute time and energy to this process | O | O | O | O |
| Staff members are willing to contribute information | O | O | O | O |
| The organizational climate suggests that people would be candid in their assessment of the organization | O | O | O | O |
| It would not be difficult to get volunteer employee participants | O | O | O | O |
| Staff members would be open to feedback about the organization and its performance | O | O | O | O |
| Managers are willing to allow their staff to participate | O | O | O | O |

Worksheet #9

# Chapter 3

# Planning the Assessment

This chapter examines the process for determining the scope of the assessment, including the decision-making process related to addressing the organization as a whole. An area of emphasis is the flexibility organizations have in examining component parts of organizations or overall assessments. It explores options for conducting an assessment, including staging, or selecting parts of the organization based on factors including leadership support, geographic location, or participant availability. This chapter examines assessment models ranging from Public Sector Assessment Improvement (PSAI) and Baldrige to a basic Strengths, Weaknesses, Opportunities, and Threats (SWOT) analysis. It addresses the implementation methods available, and considers how to select a methodology based on available staffing and available time.

Tools include:

- Assessment Scope Worksheet (#10)
- Assessment Planning Checklist (#11)

When a public sector organization decides to engage in a self-assessment process, the goal is to produce a realistic understanding of the agency's current strengths and opportunities for improvement, along with agreement on the actions that can be taken to move the organization forward and improve its ability to achieve its mission. Once a decision has been made that the organization is ready to undertake an assessment, the next step, as shown in Figure 3.1, is to plan the implementation. Planning for an assessment includes:

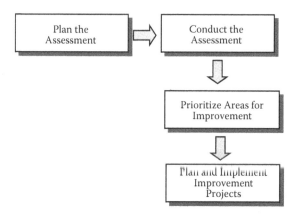

**Figure 3.1 Organizational Assessment Process diagram.**

- Defining the scope of the process
- Selecting an assessment model
- Choosing an implementation method for applying the model
- Identifying an individual or team to lead the efforts
- Identifying and preparing the people who will participate

These choices should be carefully considered. Assessments can vary in scope and depth, depending on the needs and resources of the organization and the level of involvement of the workforce. They range from very basic, less structured models to others that are more formally structured.

# Define the Scope of the Assessment

## *Organizational Components*

The first step in the planning process is to define what the organizational scope of the assessment will be, or, in other words, what part of the organization will take part in and/or be covered by the assessment. The scope of participation in an assessment process can vary greatly, depending on the agency, the particular reasons for the assessment, the resources available to conduct the assessment, and the time that can be devoted to it. Is the intention to assess the entire organization; for example, an entire agency? Or do you intend to limit the process to a section of the organization, such as a division, office, department, or a center?

The greatest potential benefit comes from assessing the entire organization in one assessment process or cycle. Examining the entire organization lets you gain an agency-wide perspective on core functions and work processes. It also has the potential to create new linkages between different parts of the organization and individuals who may not have the opportunity to interact in their normal work operations. Sharing knowledge and information from across different parts of the agency and among people with different perspectives has the potential to create new knowledge. It allows you to look at the organization as a whole, and consider the impact each part of the operation has on the others, as well as the impact that any improvements will have on the organization.

While this may be the ideal, it may not realistically be possible or practical at a given point in time. The same factors that were considered when evaluating the readiness of the organization as a whole also can be applied to determine the readiness of individual areas. There may be a number of reasons that would cause an agency to consider limiting the scope of the assessment to a portion rather than an entire agency, including:

■ The agency has multiple locations with geographically dispersed offices: Depending on the format chosen for the assessment, the process may require frequent meetings at central locations. If this is the case, an organization with multiple offices that are not within a reasonable distance of each other may find it difficult to provide access to the process to all employees and allow staff from all locations to be active participants. While this is not insurmountable (see Overcoming Obstacles to Participation boxed below), it could provide a reason to initially limit an assessment process to the offices or functions at a particular geographic location.

■ Diverse activities and constituent groups: If staff members in different parts of the agency deal with significantly different activities or constituent groups, with little interaction across divisional lines, it may make sense to assess these areas on their own. Consider, however, that there are not likely to be many parts of the organization that don't have at least some contact with other areas.

■ Different parts of the organization have different peak activity seasons: Timing can be critical and availability may differ for different parts of the agency. For example, in a public works area, the summer may be the most active time for those involved in construction, while participation during the winter might be impractical for those involved in snow removal.

■ The level of management support may differ from area to area: Is there consistent management support for the idea of an assessment across the entire organization? If not, is there a higher level of support in one or more areas? When assessing readiness for participation, it may become clear that one part of the organization is prepared to engage in this type of self-consideration, where others are not. It's not unusual for different managers or leaders to feel more or less comfortable in supporting this type of process.

■ Insufficient resources: For whatever reason, certain areas may be critically short of resources. For example, one area may have been more heavily impacted than others by an early retirement exodus or may have lost a critical grant.

■ Different levels of readiness and/or receptivity: It also can be possible for the organizational climate in one part of the organization to be less than ideal, meaning that the likelihood of positive employee participation is not as strong as other areas. This could be true if an area has been subject to a layoff or is dealing with a leadership transition or crisis.

Whatever the reason, the inability to assess the entire organization at one time should not preclude the managers of individual divisions, offices, or other units from undertaking their own assessment process, or preclude higher level managers from encouraging units they see as sufficiently ready to proceed (Figure 3.2). In this case, it may be best to use one area as a pilot group to test out the assessment process and provide positive feedback on the experience to other areas.

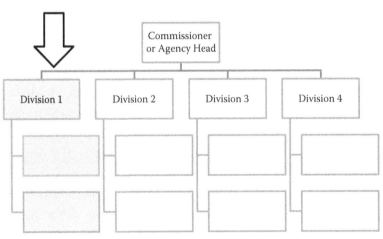

**Figure 3.2 Limited assessment based on structure. In this example, Division 1 is undertaking an assessment process. This might be an independent process, which is not expected to extend beyond this division. The agency head also may choose to treat this as a pilot program, using the experience gained and successes achieved to build support for and encourage assessments in the other divisions.**

## *Topic Areas*

Another decision to be made when evaluating the scope of the assessment is identifying the topics to be considered. In any complex organization, there are innumerable "things" that can be analyzed and studied. An effective assessment process focuses on those things that have the greatest impact on the way in which the organization functions. The planning consideration is whether the assessment will cover all the potential categories of things to be assessed.

For all the same reasons that an organization might decide to assess only certain parts of an agency, they also might decide to perform an assessment only on a limited number (one or more) of cross-functional categories. For example, if through the initial assessment readiness evaluation or preliminary planning the agency determines that there is insufficient time or resources available to complete a full assessment, they might instead focus on one or two categories that appear most important in moving the agency forward, or those most in need—because of a crisis or perceived problem—of evaluation. Using the categories in the Public Sector Assessment and Improvement model as an example (Figure 3.3), they may decide to focus on the workforce if employee morale or engagement is perceived to need attention. Strategic planning might be selected if leaders perceive that there is a problem with having common goals. In such a case, the organization can follow up at a later time with the remainder of the categories—one at a time, or together. A small agency or agency with limited resources might

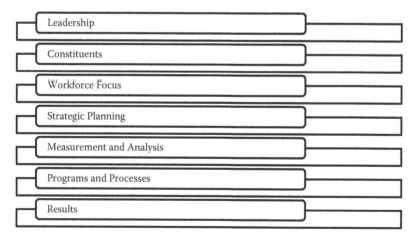

**Figure 3.3   The seven cross-functional categories that make up the Public Sector Assessment and Improvement model are each potential subject areas. A limited assessment may focus on one or more of these categories.**

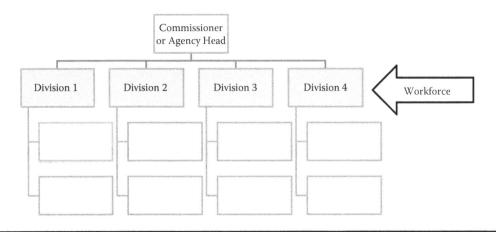

**Figure 3.4 Limited assessment based on topic/focus area. In this example, the agency has decided to limit the scope of the assessment to focus on workplace/staff issues. Drawing information from each area of the organization, the assessment will examine the whole organization's approach to its workforce, but will not examine the other potential assessment topics.**

decide to implement assessment by reviewing and focusing attention on one category each year (Figure 3.4).

The **Assessment Scope Worksheet** (page 67) can be used to determine what issues should be addressed in determining the scope of an assessment at a particular point in time.

## OVERCOMING OBSTACLES TO PARTICIPATION

If the organization includes multiple geographic locations, both the method chosen and technology can help foster across-the-board participation. Rather than use a workshop format where people might have to travel to a central location, it might be more practical to use a team-based format where people from each office collect information about their location and forward it to a central team for consolidation.

Another option might be to use technology, such as teleconferencing, to permit people from various locations to be part of the discussion, negotiation, and consensus-building stages. One of the difficulties in working through digital or virtual workgroups is that it's more difficult to build the type of trust needed to support candid discussions in a virtual environment. Leaders can overcome this through careful planning, and by encouraging discussion that allows team members to know each other; for example, by creating a virtual water cooler that encourages people to exchange information. Having a face-to-face kickoff meeting can help virtual teams build the trust necessary for effective work. Assigning prework or reading material in advance also can help start everyone off on common footing. If there are concerns about whether consistent management support for assessment exists across the agency, a smaller unit can be used as a pilot to demonstrate the process and benefits to the remaining parts of the organization and build support for future efforts.

# Choosing an Assessment Model

While the overall goal of identifying the strengths and areas for improvement may remain the same, there are many different process models available for assessment. They range in structure from less formal methods of assessment, which rely on collecting and reporting input from employees, leaders, and constituents, to more formally structured, comprehensive assessment methods, which include specific processes to direct the type of information to be collected and the manner in which it is obtained and applied. Each model differs somewhat in the factors or topics it considers and the specific questions to be asked. Of particular importance in the planning process is the degree to which any model fits the needs and the culture of the organization.

## Information Gathering Models

### Less Structured Models

Examples of simple assessments might involve a brief survey of employees and/or constituents, interviews, focus groups, or very often a SWOT (strengths, weaknesses, opportunities, and threats) analysis. The SWOT analysis is not generally limited to any particular categories, but instead considers information about any process, anticipated event or situation, workforce issue, or other information that is perceived as fitting into one of those areas. A SWOT analysis also can be used as an introduction to assessment by providing a limited analysis that gets people to think about what the issues are facing the organization.

## Structured Self-Assessment Models

Structured self-assessment models generally include both processes for assessment and a set of specific cross-functional categories or subject areas to be addressed. The identification of specific assessment topics serves as a way to focus the attention of the participants, as well as those who review the outcomes, on the areas that will make the most difference in improving operations. These categories are often broken down into a format that uses a series of questions to identify the information the organization will need for the assessment. This type of format provides a road map of important considerations (although models may differ on which factors they emphasize) and a framework for review and analysis that provides a comprehensive examination of agency operations.

## The Baldrige National Quality Award Program[1]

Baldrige is one of the most widely used and recognizable self-assessment tools in the world today and is acknowledged as a leader in defining quality. The Baldrige model focuses on products and processes, customers, leadership and governance, workforce, and finance and markets.[2] Each of these categories contains a series of questions, which collectively make up the *Criteria for Performance Excellence.* A key philosophical component of the Baldrige Program is the presumption that these criteria identify the qualities associated with excellence in organizations regardless of the type of organization in which they are found, and many research studies have demonstrated the validity of this approach.

While the most well-known use of the Baldrige criteria is as the application for the prestigious Malcolm Baldrige National Quality Award, many organizations participate in the assessment, review, and formal feedback phases without any expectation that they will contend for an award. Still others use the Baldrige criteria and methodology to conduct an internal self-assessment.

The Baldrige process has much to contribute to the assessment of government organizations. Paul Borawski, executive director and chief strategic officer of the American Society for Quality, describes the way that the Baldrige Award has contributed to quality in the public sector by saying:

> Quality has several definitions depending on the context of its use; two seem particularly fit when thinking of public service: quality is the least cost to society [and] quality is the systematic pursuit of excellence. They are complementary and supportive definitions.

The first speaks of the "what." What a consumer (citizen) expects—that a company, or government, deliver its product/service at the lowest possible cost to society. This entails efficiency and effectiveness, the elimination of waste and considerations of the societal costs as well; sustainability and social responsibility. The second definition speaks of the "how." The only way an organization can make progress against the first definition is by adopting concepts, techniques, and tools that help turn their good intentions into actions and results. The Malcolm Baldrige National Quality Award provides a comprehensive model for any organization to use in determining their strengths and opportunities and examining the fundamentals of excellence. Award recipients provide evidence of the obtainments of "best practice" performance and models of success for others to emulate. Government recipients of a Baldrige award provide proof that the "best in government" equals the performance of the "best in business." Society is the benefactor.[3]

The Baldrige program has adapted its own model to address the needs of other sectors. Its success and worldwide adoption in the for-profit business sector resulted in the development of customized versions for the health-care industry and for education. In 2007, the Baldrige program opened its existing business-based Criteria for Performance Excellence to the nonprofit sector (charities, trade and professional associations, and government agencies) adjusting some of the language and descriptions to include concepts more familiar to the public sector. That year, Coral Springs, Florida, became the first municipality to win the Baldrige award. The U.S. Army Armament Research Development and Engineering Center (ARDEC) became the first federal agency to do so.

The Baldrige criteria for healthcare reflect two other concepts that are important for the public sector. In addition to an emphasis on patient-focused excellence, it calls attention to the multilevel legal and regulatory environment that exists in the healthcare industry and the need to consider not only current patients, but also to anticipate future community health needs (Baldrige, 2007c), which is consistent with the community-based planning that takes place in government organizations. It also specifically addresses the idea that it is not possible that all patients will have the desired outcome; despite the best care, some patients will continue to have significant healthcare problems. Similarly, some constituents in the public sector also will not have the desired outcomes. Government is placed in the spot of making decisions about actions in the best interests of society, even if those are not the outcomes desired by all. Consider as an example the issue of eminent domain where government agencies take private property for a public good, such as school construction or community development.

## The Balanced Scorecard

In 1992, Drs. Robert Kaplan and David Norton of Harvard University introduced the Balanced Scorecard model. Their self-described purpose was to add "strategic nonfinancial performance measures to existing financial metrics to give managers and executives a more balanced view of organizational performance."[4] They recognized that the traditional emphasis on measuring financial performance in the private sector did not present a complete picture that would account for the performance of excellent organizations. The original model included four areas—financial, customer, internal business processes, and learning and growth—and businesses were challenged to select measures in each of these areas.

In 1996, the City of Charlotte, North Carolina, became the first municipality to use a balanced scorecard system to align its vision for the city with the roles and responsibilities of its government. An article in *Government Finance Review* (Eagle, 2004) describes the evolution of Charlotte's system, which began with measuring outcomes and changed to a balanced scorecard approach. Charlotte was "ready to move beyond measuring mere outputs to a system that would provide actionable data on efficiency and effectiveness."[5] The State of Utah introduced a balanced scorecard approach to performance management in 2006 in an effort to improve overall government performance, using outcome-based measures that tie into the state's strategic plan and allow each agency to track its performance against key performance indicators.

## *Structured Assessment Processes Adapted for the Public Sector*

When choosing from existing models, it is important to evaluate the applicability of each model to government. Models designed for the private sector may not match public sector practices, although they can be customized by the using agency. For assessment to be effective and gain the understanding and participation of the workforce, it must begin with a solid assessment framework that is adapted—in terms of language, information, and key components—to government's unique needs. Many of the factors used to assess the performance and operation of government are the same as those used in other sectors, but it also is important to recognize the differences, and to look for opportunities to speak specifically to the experiences of public employees. By making some simple changes in language, and adding different definitions of success, agencies can adapt assessment models to recognize the realities of the public sector. Alternatively, government agencies may decide to use tools that are adapted specifically for the public sector.

## THE IMPORTANCE OF PUBLIC SECTOR PRACTICES IN SELECTING ASSESSMENT MODELS

Two examples of practices that require different definitions of process and different measures of success are financial measures and human resources. There are distinct differences in the relative importance of financial measures in the two sectors. For the most part, government does not use the same bottom line, profit-oriented financial metrics. Although there are, increasingly, examples of entrepreneurial government, the majority of federal, state, and local agencies are not financially self-supporting. Younis (1997) describes the disincentives to financial responsibility that exist in many public agencies by pointing out: "The annual financing of public sector services produces a culture where it is prudent not to demonstrate savings, but to emphasize lack of finances in the hope that more will be available next time."[6] In agencies charged with distributing funds to communities or to other levels of government, success might be defined as having exhausted all of your available funding. A remaining balance at the end of the fiscal year is often interpreted to mean that the program had too much money to start with, and the result can often be a reduction in next year's allocation. The need to provide services to society as a whole means that government will always have functions that will have difficulty being economically self-supporting, such as public transportation. Government also does not have the prerogative that the private sector does to eliminate unprofitable programs. What this means is that the results section of an assessment model needs to be structured in a way that emphasizes factors other than financial measures as the primary methods of defining success. In the area of human resources, many government agencies work within merit systems and regulations that may preclude certain practices used in the private sector, and whose limitations bring with them the need for different human resource models and practices. Although performance management is very important, pay-for-performance systems are difficult to implement in public agencies, as are bonuses and other types of financial rewards. Constituents are often critical of what they perceive to be excessive overtime payments, without completely understanding the need to provide some services without regard to staffing shortages.

In his work on diffusion of innovation, Everett Rogers (1995) suggests that the likelihood that a new idea will be accepted depends on the degree to which the innovation meets certain qualities. Two of those qualities, compatibility and complexity, are particularly important in understanding the need to adapt assessment models to fit the public sector. Compatibility is defined by Rogers as the degree to which an idea is compatible with the values and experiences of those faced with adopting it. Complexity refers to the degree of perceived difficulty in understanding. The question is the degree to which the model chosen reflects the values and experiences of the public sector, which would increase the likelihood of its acceptance. Using terminology and examples that reflect the experiences of public sector employees makes it more likely that an assessment model and process will meet the test of compatibility and complexity.

The Public Sector Assessment and Improvement (PSAI) model, which is discussed in detail in this workbook, is grounded in the Baldrige categories, but extends it by adapting it to meet the language and culture of the public sector.[7] The PSAI model was designed specifically for use in the public sector, based on the understanding that the best assessment tool for government agencies is one that acknowledges the purposes, functions, culture, and language that is integral to the way they function.[8] The PSAI model is made up of seven categories (Figure 3.5), each representing an area in which any public sector organization must demonstrate effectiveness. Combined, they provide a roadmap for achieving excellent performance. Each of the seven categories is significant, but the relationships between the categories also have implications for understanding the operation of government organizations.

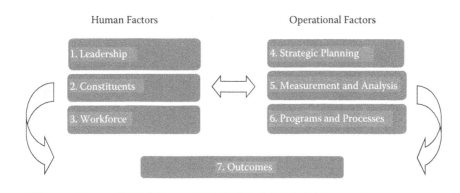

Human Factors                                    Operational Factors

1. Leadership                          4. Strategic Planning

2. Constituents                       5. Measurement and Analysis

3. Workforce                          6. Programs and Processes

7. Outcomes

**Figure 3.5   The Public Sector Assessment and Improvement model.**

# Choosing an Implementation Method

Once a model has been chosen, the next step is to identify an implementation method. While the choice of model influences what topics are covered and what questions are used for collecting information, the word *method* refers to the way in which the actual assessment process is conducted: how the information is collected, by whom, and how it is used. The decision depends to a large degree on how the overall effort is envisioned. Is this intended to be a short-term (or one-time) effort, or a long-term effort? Is the intent to collect information or to build relationships? Is the goal to produce general awareness of the workings of the organization, or to create a document for review and distribution? At one end of a possible continuum of options are efforts where a few people conduct an extensive data-gathering effort, study the information, and write a report for use by a leadership group. At the other end of the continuum are retreat efforts where the emphasis is on engagement and increased self-awareness rather than documentation. Most efforts fall somewhere between the two, but all of these factors influence the method of assessment selected. It becomes a way of identifying the importance of and balance between these factors (Figure 3.6).

## Balancing the Available Time Frame with the Available Resources

Although there may be other considerations, the choice of a method depends in large part on two factors: (1) the length of time available to conduct an assessment and (2) the human resources—the number of people available and willing to serve as participants in the process.

Selecting an appropriate assessment model requires that leaders understand and respect the resources available. Realistically, any assessment

- Number of people involved
- Time
- Amount of information
- Employee learning
- Ownership
- Level of engagement

**Figure 3.6  Factors to balance.**

process will involve an investment of time and human resources.[9] The required amount can vary, which impacts the depth and thoroughness of the effort. Determining the available time frame differs from identifying whether a particular point in time is feasible. The available time frame is the length of time for which the resources of the agency can be devoted to assessment, a judgment based on the amount of time organizational leaders are willing to have those resources diverted. The time frame for an assessment process can span days, weeks, or months. A short, focused assessment process may take no longer than a day. An in-depth, extensive process can take much longer, sometimes as much as a year or more. Another consideration is that, while it takes more time, a more extensive process can create broad-based engagement and ownership of the results.

Balancing available time against available staff members is a "chicken or egg" question. If the realities of the workload limit the number of available participants, it would not be a good idea to select a more complex or extensive method that requires the participation of a large number of people. This is a particularly difficult issue in many organizations, such as corrections or social work agencies that may be chronically short staffed and that do not have periods of time that would be considered "down" time. Also customer service, whether the "customer" is an inmate or an applicant for a license; the nature of the work prohibits time away from the assigned work area. The time available to participate might vary by program area or by occupational group. It becomes a question of who has the time to participate and the perceived importance of including different groups and levels. The people at the highest levels may have the least available time, and yet their participation can be critical to a successful process. If an active participation model is used, and there are a number of groups with significant

:ime limitations, it may be possible to incorporate passive participation from :hose groups as part of the overall process.

The selection of an assessment model also depends on the level of orga-nizational commitment for the process. If there is limited commitment, then .t is unlikely that resources will be available for an extensive assessment pro-:ess. In this situation, a simpler method of assessment will provide at least some information. If this process is well received, it can serve as a starting point for more in-depth assessment later on.

## Methods

There may be as many different methods of assessment as there are govern-ment agencies willing to try them. However, there are four primary meth-ods that can be adapted for use in any organization. They represent various combinations of time and resource needs, and the decision of which to use must be made by each agency based on their circumstances at that time Figure 3.7).

Simply stated, the best process at any given time is one that balances the mprovement needs of the organization with the available resources.

The four methods that will be discussed include surveys, workshops, project teams, and organization-wide teams (Figure 3.8).

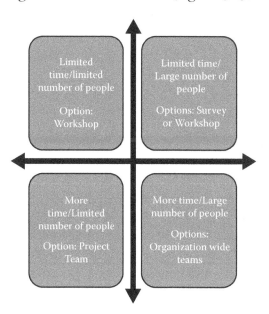

**Figure 3.7** The choice of an assessment method depends on the amount of time and the available staff resources. Different methods can be best in different situations.

☐ Implementation Methods

☐ Surveys

☐ Workshops

☐ Project Teams

☐ Organization-wide Teams

**Figure 3.8  The four primary implementation methods. These methods can be used with any assessment model.**

## Survey

A simple way to conduct a very basic assessment is to survey employees. Using a paper or Web-based survey tool, staff members can be asked to identify the strengths and opportunities for improvement that they perceive, either in the organization as a whole, the section in which they work, or both. A survey also can contain the questions associated with a more structured model, including Baldrige or PSAI. A well-designed survey with an appropriate distribution method can provide access to the entire organization, and as a result, collect information from all program areas and demographic groups.

One consideration, though, is that because completion of a workplace survey is generally not mandatory, the response rate can vary widely from area to area and group to group. This can impact whether the information received reflects the views of a true cross section and, accordingly, can impact the applicability of the information across the organization. Surveys can also be distributed to a random sample of employees, which might again impact the information that can be obtained. Surveys can be used as well to collect similar information from constituents. Once the information is collected and the results are compiled, the information can be used, most likely by management, to develop action plans and priorities for improvement.

The main drawback to using surveys as an assessment method is that while they have the potential for agency-wide involvement, they do not provide an opportunity for interaction, including information exchange, negotiation, and consensus building. It may not be feasible to engage survey participants in setting priorities for identified improvement opportunities, although this can be done by means of a follow-up survey in which they could rank identified areas for improvement. While the collection of data using a survey can potentially involve large numbers of employees, someone still needs to do the analysis and decide what to do with the information.

The advantage of using surveys is that they enable the organization to get information from a broader group of participants than could physically be incorporated into the process. In an agency of 5,000 people, it's not likely that everyone can or will want to be involved. This becomes a way to engage people who might not otherwise express interest in participation or have the opportunity to participate. A survey also can be a first step in a more structured assessment process as a means to gather information. It can be used to gather preliminary information; for example, in a large organization, a survey can be used to find out what the commonly held beliefs are about the need for improvement so that subsequent efforts can be more focused.

## Workshop

A facilitated workshop is a popular method of conducting an organizational assessment. Generally lasting from one to two full days, a workshop allows an assessment process to take place with a relatively small, focused investment of time and resources. A workshop often uses trained facilitators, drawn either from inside or outside the agency, to guide participants through a review of the categories or topics to be assessed. A workshop can be conducted onsite or offsite. For each category, the participants exchange the information that they bring from their personal experience and organizational knowledge and then develop a list of the strengths and areas for improvement in each category. The last step in the workshop process is to prioritize the areas for improvement and select projects for future action. The disadvantage of the workshop method is that the participants may not have all the information needed to fully respond to the questions in each category. Because of the time allowed and the structure of the workshop, there is no opportunity in this model for them to seek out or research additional information. The time frame also limits the amount of time to discuss and review the information.

The extent to which the staff and leaders can participate in this process depends largely on the size of the organization. This concentrated model is often a good way for a small agency or unit to include the entire staff. Workshops can include as few as 10 or as many as 100 people. One benefit for smaller agencies is that by including everyone in a single workshop, the information is shared with all staff members at the same time and everyone becomes part of the assessment process. In larger agencies, the size limitations may require the use of a representative group of people to provide information from different areas. Alternatively, multiple workshops can be held to include a larger proportion of the workforce, and the information obtained from each consolidated to form a more complete picture.

## Project Team

A project team is made up of a limited number of employee participants who are chosen or who volunteer to undertake the assessment process on behalf of the agency. The project team can be any size, but should be representative of the different employee groups or areas to be assessed. Those identified as team members are responsible for managing the overall project, which includes identifying how and from whom information is collected. Project teams typically meet on a predetermined schedule over a period of days, weeks, or months. An advantage that a project team has over either surveys or workshops is that it is not limited to the existing information each member possesses nor to asking just once for that information. Project teams can collect and compare information, evaluate it, conduct additional research as needed, and tap multiple sources. A potential disadvantage of a project team is that the process might be seen as "belonging" to those individuals and not the workforce as a whole. To counteract this, the project team needs to employ various communication strategies to keep the workforce as a whole involved and engaged in the process and to build interest in the assessment outcomes.

## Organization-Wide Team

This method has, for larger agencies in particular, the broadest possible level of participation of those presented here. It involves selecting a project coordinator or coordinating team, which then creates a large team of participants, representative of each area and discipline in the agency. The participants are divided into smaller teams, with each subteam assigned one or more of the assessment categories (Figure 3.9). Each team is charged with collecting the information on its category from across the organization and, like project teams, has the ability to conduct research to get the best possible information from a wide number of perspectives concerning its category. The team can then take the information and develop a list of the strengths and opportunities for improvement and can prepare an analysis to be shared with the other teams to create a collective picture of the organization.

| Team 1 | Leadership | Team 4 | Strategic Planning |
| Team 2 | Constituents | Team 5 | Measurement and Analysis |
| Team 3 | Workforce | Team 6 | Programs and Processes |

**Figure 3.9   Sample distribution of subgroup assignments.**

| Method | Information Collection | Information Exchange | Negotiation and Consensus | Improvement Plan Development | Agency-wide Involvement |
|---|---|---|---|---|---|
| Survey | Medium | Low | Low | Low | High |
| Workshop | Medium | High | High | High | High-Low |
| Project Team | High | High | High | High | Low |
| Organization-wide Team | High | High | High | High | Medium-High |

**Figure 3.10   Comparison of the level of involvement for each method based on the stages of assessment.**

A potential problem with the use of organization-wide teams is that they may overlap in their information-seeking process and may ask the same people for information. A more serious concern would be that teams assigned to each assessment category may have less of an opportunity to gain an overall sense of the assessment-wide information, because they are focused on only one topic. However, these potential limitations are really dependent on how the process is conducted and a good project coordinator or coordinating team can find ways to integrate the information and to include all the category-based teams in the review of all the material.

As shown in Figure 3.10, each of these methods varies in the level of staff involvement in the assessment process.

## Identifying an Individual or Team to Lead the Effort

Choosing a process leader can be critically important to the success of the assessment. While assessment can be and frequently is a team effort, it requires day-to-day leadership to establish direction, oversee process, negotiate agreements, establish priorities, and measure progress against planned schedules.

Ideally, the person chosen will possess certain characteristics:

■ Thorough knowledge of the organization being assessed
■ Good interpersonal and communication skills
■ Project management ability
■ Familiarity with the assessment model and methodology

The most important qualification is an interest in the process and the opportunity to improve the organization. The organizational level of the person selected is less important than the ability to generate interest and sustain involvement among diverse staff groups.

Key to the success of the project and the effectiveness of the process leader is a clear understanding of the decision-making structure. Will the process leader have the responsibility and the authority to make decisions on the conduct of the assessment? Will decisions be made by organizational leaders and implemented by the process leader? This is especially important in the planning phase where organizational leaders must be in concert with the operational plans for the assessment.

## Using a Trained Facilitator

Many organizations use professionally trained facilitators to support the assessment process. They can come from inside the agency or can be external professional or academic consultants or organizational development professionals. The decision to use facilitators is based in large part on the chosen assessment method and model. If the method selected for the process involves work in teams, either as an ongoing process or as a workshop, then it is particularly helpful to have someone facilitate the workshop or meetings so that they do not get bogged down and to ensure that every area gets sufficient consideration. Organization staff members who are going to be in charge of teams also could benefit from training as facilitators.

What is the role of the facilitator? The facilitator in an assessment has several very important roles. First, the facilitator serves as an educator by:

■ educating the participants about the chosen assessment model and how it is used

- explaining the terminology of assessment and creating a common vocabulary
- providing information about the purpose of assessment and the specific goals for the process

Second, the facilitator serves as a moderator by:

- ensuring that all participants have the opportunity and a process through which they can participate
- challenging participants to develop information to support their perceptions
- making sure that all categories to be assessed and all areas under assessment receive appropriate attention

## Communicate Plans for the Assessment

Sharing information about the assessment process is a theme that begins in the planning process and runs through all stages, methods, and models. It serves a very important purpose in preparing the organization for the assessment. Candid and ongoing communication provides a way to engage people who may not actually participate in the process. The messages that go out to staff members—by email, memo, or in person through meetings and discussions—should inform people about what will happen and what they should expect to see. It prepares them for any projected contributions of time, information, and effort. Most important, providing such information throughout the planning process in advance of the actual process has the benefit of counteracting concern and possible misinformation about the purpose of the assessment. Organizational leaders and process leaders need to address the motivations of the agency up front. If the assessment is being undertaken to improve internal operations or the way that services are provided to constituents, communicate that to them, so people don't perceive that it is being done in anticipation of downsizing or solely for the purpose of reorganization.

The **Assessment Planning Checklist** (page 69) can be used to record planning decisions made and to ensure that all decision points have been considered.

# Endnotes

1. Information about the Baldrige National Quality Program is available at www. Baldrige.org
2. NIST Web site: http://www.nist.gov/baldrige/publications/bus_about.cfm
3. Email communication from Paul Borawski, American Society for Quality (June 27, 2008).
4. Balanced Scorecard Institute: http://www.balancedscorecard.org
5. Eagle, K. (2004) p. 19.
6. Younis (1997) p. 123.
7. The PSAI model is based on the Baldrige Criteria for Performance Excellence, and replicates its format of seven categories under which a series of questions (called the criteria) describe the information that will provide the inputs for assessing the organization. It also draws on other assessment models, particularly *Excellence in Higher Education* (Ruben, 2010), which adapts the Baldrige criteria to the language and culture of higher education.
8. Other processes also have adapted the Baldrige criteria, for example, at the state level, Florida's Sterling Award.
9. This book defines assessment as a self-assessment conducted by members of the organization, which by definition requires an investment of time and human resources. Organizations also have the option to hire a consultant to conduct an assessment, but even this requires an investment of time and resources, because the people in the organization are the ones who have the knowledge and access to the information required.

# Assessment Scope Worksheet

This worksheet is designed to provide a framework for discussing the scope of an organizational self-assessment process. It considers whether the organization would benefit from a full assessment of all areas or whether an assessment that is more limited in scope would be more beneficial at this point in time. It also considers possible topics of assessment and asks whether the full range or a sample of the potential topics would be more feasible.

## 1. Please indicate whether the following statements are true for all areas of the organization, true for most areas, true for some areas, or not true.

| | True for all | True for most | True for some | Not true at all |
|---|---|---|---|---|
| The geographic distribution of our offices could preclude people from participating | ○ | ○ | ○ | ○ |
| Technology is an available resource for overcoming issues of geographic location | ○ | ○ | ○ | ○ |
| We can provide ways for staff members from all locations to participate | ○ | ○ | ○ | ○ |
| Primary constituents are the same or very similar across the organization | ○ | ○ | ○ | ○ |
| Each part of the organization interacts with all other parts | ○ | ○ | ○ | ○ |
| Different parts of the organization have different peak activity seasons | ○ | ○ | ○ | ○ |
| Staff members from all parts of the organization could be available to work on this process at the same time | ○ | ○ | ○ | ○ |
| There is consistent management support for an assessment across the organization | ○ | ○ | ○ | ○ |
| Available resources are distributed evenly to all areas | ○ | ○ | ○ | ○ |
| The lack of resources in some areas could prohibit their participation | ○ | ○ | ○ | ○ |
| Staff members would be receptive to participation | ○ | ○ | ○ | ○ |
| Staff morale could impact willingness to participate | ○ | ○ | ○ | ○ |

## 2. Please indicate your level of agreement with the following statements:

| | Strongly agree | Agree | Disagree | Strongly disagree |
|---|---|---|---|---|
| At the current time, the best idea is to have all parts of the organization participate | ○ | ○ | ○ | ○ |
| At the current time, the best idea is to limit participation to certain areas | ○ | ○ | ○ | ○ |
| At the current time, the best idea is to limit participation to one area in particular | ○ | ○ | ○ | ○ |
| At the current time, the best idea is to identify an area willing to serve as a pilot | ○ | ○ | ○ | ○ |

Worksheet #10

## Assessment Scope Worksheet

**3. How important are each of the following potential topics to an assessment process at this time?**

| | Very important | Somewhat important | Important | Less important | Not importar |
|---|---|---|---|---|---|
| Leadership | O | O | O | O | O |
| Constituents | O | O | O | O | O |
| Workforce | O | O | O | O | O |
| Strategic Planning | O | O | O | O | O |
| Measurement and Analysis | O | O | O | O | O |
| Processes and Programs | O | O | O | O | O |
| Outcomes | O | O | O | O | O |

**4. Please indicate your level of agreement with the following statements:**

| | Strongly agree | Agree | Disagree | Strongly disagree |
|---|---|---|---|---|
| At the current time, the best idea is to include all assessment cateories | O | O | O | O |
| At the current time, the best idea is to limit the assessment to certain categories | O | O | O | O |
| At the current time, the best idea is to limit the assessment to only one category | O | O | O | O |

**(Continued) Worksheet #10**

# Assessment Planning Checklist

This checklist can be used to ensure that all planning areas have been discussed and decisions reached. It can also be used to record the decisions made.

## 1. Identify the organizational scope of the assessment

○ The entire agency or organization

○ Selected parts of the agency or organization

○ One organizational unit

○ One program

○ Other

If the whole organization is not participating, please identify the area(s) selected

## 2. Which topic areas will be part of the assessment process? Please check all that apply.

☐ Leadership

☐ Constituents

☐ Workforce Focus

☐ Strategic Planning

☐ Measurement and Analysis

☐ Processes and Programs

☐ Outcomes

## 3. Which assessment model will be used?

## 4. Which assessment method will be used?

○ Survey

○ Workshop

○ Project Teams

○ Organization-wide Teams

## 5. Who has been identified as the process leader(s)?

Worksheet #11

## Assessment Planning Checklist

### 6. Will a facilitator be used?

○ Yes

○ No

Please specify who will serve as the facilitator

### 7. What is the anticipated time frame for the assessment?

### 8. Who will be responsible for communication with employees?

(Continued) Worksheet #11

*Chapter 4*

# Engaging Employees in the Assessment Process

This chapter discusses the many options available to organizations in deciding how to best involve employees in the assessment effort. It considers the possible levels of engagement and how to maximize employee time and energy. It considers the best way to ensure that employees are given a common language to discuss assessment and how that can contribute toward creating change.

Tool:

■ Organizational Demographic Worksheet (#12)

## Engaging the Employees

> It is a mistake to assume we know any system's productive capacity before we involve people in shaking out the bugs.
> Marvin Weisbord (1987)[1]

Public sector organizations are very diverse, not just in terms of the people who work there, but also in terms of the occupations, professions, and disciplines that they represent. As a result, people often have very different ways of talking about what goes on in their workplace and how they get it done. It seems logical to think that people who work for the same agency, and perform activities designed to accomplish the mission and goals of that

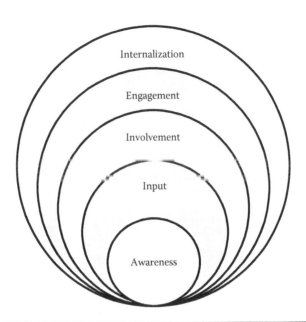

**Figure 4.1   Levels of staff involvement.**

agency would have common ways of describing the organization, its structure, its people, and its way of doing business. However, this is not always
the case, and people may not have opportunities to interact or share information with others outside their own part of the organizational structure.

One of the most critical success factors in planning the assessment is
deciding how to engage members of the organization in the process, and to
what extent they will participate. Whatever model is chosen, and whatever
scope is defined, the assessment process at some level must include the participation of the people that make up the organization. There are five levels
of employee involvement, as shown in Figure 4.1:

**Level 1: Awareness**—Staff members are introduced to and made aware
of the concept of assessment, but are not, generally speaking, actively
involved in the process.

**Level 2: Input**—Staff members are asked to provide available data and
information for use in the assessment. This may take place through a
single-directional tool, like a survey or through focus groups. While
they may be subsequently advised of the outcome, either at intervals or
at the completion, they are not active participants in the analysis and
application of the information.

**Level 3: Involvement**—Staff members are given the opportunity to
actively participate in the process by researching assessment questions

for which the answers may not be readily available. They not only contribute information, but also engage in the analysis and interpretation of the information. They may have input into how the information will be used, and help determine the assessment outcomes.

**Level 4: Engagement**—Staff members are active participants in the process of assessment, seeking out, collecting, interpreting, and applying the information. They are actively involved in decisions about the progress of the assessment process. More than just participating, staff members at this level are actively creating new information and determining outcomes and priorities.

**Level 5: Internalization**—At this level, assessment becomes part of the workforce culture. Assessment and improvement become part of the consideration for every workplace decision. The ability to assess the organization and its processes becomes a core competency for employees and a valued trait for leadership.

The first two levels (awareness and input) are called passive involvement, where the next three levels (involvement, engagement, and internalization) reflect active involvement.

The most successful assessment processes involve a broad range of individuals from across the organization in order to facilitate the broadest possible information inputs. That can present a challenge to both large and small agencies who must sustain a full range of activities while engaging in an assessment process. The trade-offs differ for large and small organizations: A large organization may be able to identify people for whom working on the assessment is a full-time assignment; a small agency may not be able to sustain services if even a few staff members are assigned full time. On the other hand, a small organization might be able to engage everyone in the agency in the process; a large agency might not find it possible or practical to involve everyone. The most important factor is to determine a balance that meets the needs of the organization and, having said that, a critical first step is to convince organizational leaders that participation in an assessment is valuable, and not just an added burden on an already burdened staff. In the long run, the goal is to establish a culture where participation in an assessment is regarded not as an "extra" activity, but as a key part of each person's responsibilities. This begins by understanding the many benefits employee participation brings to the organization. Research on assessment has documented that participants can learn a great deal about their organization

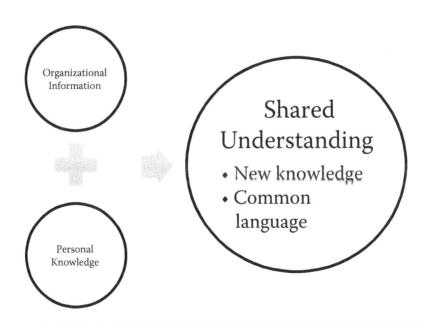

**Figure 4.2    The assessment process includes many opportunities for people to inter-act, exchange information, and create new communication relationships.**

through active engagement in an assessment process, and the most significant by-product of their participation may be improved communication across the agency.

The communication that takes place during the assessment can provide a good basis for increasing and improving the quality of communication that takes place during the ongoing daily operation of the organization. The process brings together people who may not work together on a regular basis and gives them a format to discuss their different roles and responsibilities. During the assessment process, participants develop new communication channels as they seek out information. It provides an opportunity to build links with others and for them to carry on those conversations long after the formal assessment process has ended. The process also creates interpersonal and cross-organizational working relationships (Figure 4.2). This can have lasting impacts, and can facilitate and enhance the amount, type, and level of communication that takes place in the organization long after the assessment process is completed.

## *The Importance of People in the Information Collection Process*

The process of assessing the performance and capability of the organization relies on the ability to obtain sufficient information to understand the way ir which it currently functions, and that begins with collecting information that describes current practices and results. The process of collecting the information needed depends almost completely on the contributions of employees, either through knowledge that they already possess, or through their ability to assemble the needed information. It is both a research project and a learning process for those who take part.

Information collection of this kind requires participants to find, bring together, and exchange information from all parts of the workplace in order to create a complete description of the current state of the organization. This, in turn, requires that people from across the organization be involved in the information-collection process. Why is it so important to include a cross section of people? Simply put, it's not possible for any one person, regardless of his/her job, rank, longevity, or location to know everything that there is to know about the workings of the organization. Much of the information needed to conduct an assessment already exists within the organization, but not necessarily in a form that is readily known by all or easily available. The information can reside in many locations, based on the function or unit where the work takes place, and exist in many different forms: written, verbal, electronic, and visual. It can include data and statistics, written reports, flow charts, and stories about practices. Think of the vast quantities of information that are present in every organization. This information is generated every day in the course of doing business, but it may be known only to those people involved in a specific program or procedure. The success of the information collection stage relies heavily on involving people who know about and have access to different pools of information. For that reason, the best results can be achieved by engaging a diverse group of participants with access to different parts of the organization and different types of knowledge.[2]

During the course of compiling and exchanging this information, the participants will, without question, find that while they know a lot about their agency, some of the assumptions and beliefs that they have about their workplace may not be completely accurate, or may not reflect the whole story of the agency. They may begin to challenge some of their own beliefs or those of co-workers. Instead of relying on individual experiences alone, the assessment process allows them to compare their individual knowledge and information with that provided by co-participants, which increases the scope and depth of knowledge they have about the organization.

## *Identifying Participating Groups and Individual Participants*

The next step is to determine who will participate in the process. The assessment method chosen will determine, to a large degree, the number of participants who will be required. While some organizations may have the ability to include every employee in the information collection stage, either because the agency is small enough to do so (for example, having every employee participate in a workshop-model assessment, or by surveying every employee), others will not. The most successful assessment processes will include participants at all stages that reflect the demographic makeup of the organization, because the required knowledge resides with people at all levels. But, who should be included? There are several ways to approach selecting the participants (Figure 4.3).

There are different occupational groups, such as managers, professionals, and technical and administrative staff, who all have different perspectives and different ways of looking at and describing their workplace. There are specialists with jobs and functions that support the core technical mission (for example, social work, health, or environmental science), but also in the many other disciplines necessary for them to operate effectively, such as accounting, records management, or grant administration. Some government agencies may have librarians or mechanics and fleet managers. There are experts, that is, the person who knows everything about a particular area or process. This can

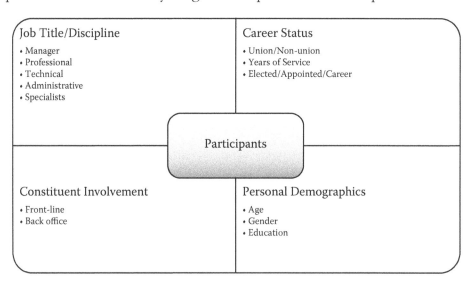

**Figure 4.3   When considering who to include, the demographics of the organization can be examined many ways. This matrix considers some of the job and personal characteristics.**

include the "go to" person, as in "Ask Mary, she knows all about that" or "John is the only one who understands how that works." That person may have very specific knowledge about his/her role, but may not understand how his/her particular process (or piece of a larger process) fits into the overall scheme of things. There are also experts who have specialized knowledge about a field of endeavor that may be relatively isolated in the organization. Another consideration is career status, which can include union/nonunion designations, groups based on years of service, and career employees, political appointees, and elected officials. Different perspectives can certainly be obtained from those who have significant constituent involvement, such as your front-line staff and those with only internal constituents. Last and certainly not least, it is important to consider personal demographics: age, gender, race, education level.

Because participants are empowered, enabled, and encouraged to collect information about their own area and other parts of the organization, it's also important to include people who understand the organization from a horizontal and from a vertical perspective.

## Horizontal Knowledge

One way to look at the organization is as a series of horizontal slices. In the example in Figure 4.4, administrative staff members, though they work in different areas, may have common work activities and shared practices. They may interact with each other on a regular basis in order to accomplish those processes, giving them certain knowledge that might not be available to the professional or technical staff. Similarly, they might share access to constituents that differs from the access that others have. The front-line person who has direct contact with the agencies' clients, such as the person processing registrations or driver's licenses at a motor vehicle agency or voter registration

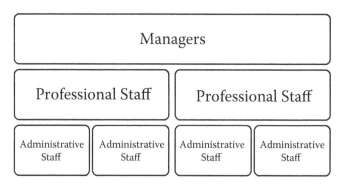

**Figure 4.4    Example of horizontal information in organizations.**

documents at a county clerk's office, has an understanding of the constituents' needs and expectations that may be very different than the information that the chief executive has. Technical staff may have information about systems and processes. A good example of this is the understanding of programming, hardware and software systems, and database management information that information technology staff members have, which may not be available to others. Senior executives who are responsible for policy decisions will have access to information on which those decisions are based, and understand the intent of the decisions. They will have information about the external environment that may not be widely known to the staff.

## Vertical Knowledge

The organization also can be considered in vertical slices. People may know a great deal about how their own division or unit works, but not about the other units that make up the agency. Unfortunately, many people are only aware of their own area, which causes them to think, act, and plan within their organizational silos.

In the example shown in Figure 4.5, someone who works in Division A of the Department of Public Works may understand what goes on in that division, but may not interact with Division B. Their organizational knowledge, therefore, is limited to the vertical structure in which they work.

It's important to realize that access to information may be limited as a result of social divisions in the workplace. Managers, professionals, laborers, technicians, and clerical staff have different levels of access to the decision-making process (Deetz, 1995). They may not have common views of the organization because they do not have the same information on which to base their conclusions. By bringing people together, assessment processes

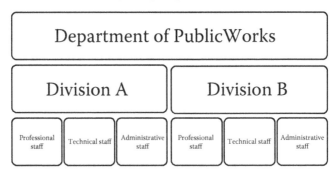

**Figure 4.5 Example of vertical knowledge.**

can help break down the barriers between those who normally have access to information and those who do not. Those who have the opportunity to participate in an assessment process may be very different than those who normally make decisions. The **Participant Demographics Worksheet** (page 85) can be used to review and consider the representation.

Once you have determined the key groups for participation, the next consideration is how individual participants are selected. In some organizations, the decision may be to use only those who volunteer for the process. While the use of volunteers might increase the likelihood of active participation, it's important to consider whether those who volunteer will be able to provide all the necessary information. You can assign people to participate, based on organizational knowledge and demographics, but they may not have the interest in the process needed to guarantee good outcomes. Ideally, the goal is to find a combination of interest and enthusiasm that will guarantee sustained participation.

It's important to note that, because of the realities of organizational life, there will be key information that resides with others who are not engaged in the process if for no other reason than their work assignment makes it impractical for them to do so. There are other methods of ensuring the participation of these key players, including having them be interviewed by assessment participants, or having them contribute documents or other material to support the effort.

Generally speaking, even if it's possible to include all employees in the information collection stage, it's likely that a subset of the organization will be used in the subsequent stages to establish priorities and complete the remaining tasks in the assessment process. Therefore, careful consideration must be given to the makeup of the participants for all stages.

## BEST PRACTICE

**Pay attention to participant demographics**—The best possible information is obtained when the knowledge and perspectives of all groups are considered and included. Therefore, it's extremely important to make sure that the participants match the demographics of the organization, in terms of major job category, union and management, ethnicity and gender, seniority/length of time with the organization, and education.

The next question is whether to integrate participation as part of the normal work performed or whether it becomes a full-time assignment. Some organizations set up organizational assessment or strategic planning offices thinking that it will be a full-time assignment. That may work well in some agencies, but it also can create a sense of distance from the process and lack of buy-in as opposed to the sense of ownership that comes from involving people across the organization. A middle ground for a project team or organization-wide project team is to temporarily assign them to the teams on a full or part-time basis.

## *Leader Participation*

A significant consideration is whether leaders—organizational leaders or the directors or managers of specific areas (Figure 4.6)—should be included in the process. The organizational leader's participation is determined in the planning stage. The leader may introduce and explain the importance of the process, and leave the work to the selected participants, or the leader may participate in a more active role, for example, by attending the workshop as a participant. The pros and cons of the leader's involvement should be thoroughly considered prior to the process. People in leadership positions have broad knowledge of the organization and can contribute information from a different perspective than those at other levels. However, the benefit of tapping their knowledge must be balanced against the impact that can result from their active participation. Think, for example, about the group dynamics that might result if a division director or lead administrator were to participate in an assessment workshop.

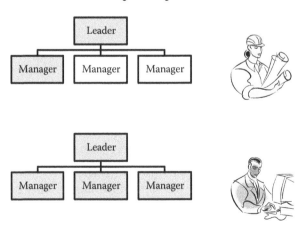

**Figure 4.6 Employees may define leaders in different ways.**

here is a possibility that their active participation can have a chilling effect on the candor of the discussion by those who work for them, especially when discussing topics such as leadership and the workforce. Leader participation has other advantages. It can create a deeper understanding of the employee perspective, allow the leader to participate in creating shared perspective, and ease the leader's ability to translate insight from the assessment into leadership initiatives for improvement. Whether or not to include leaders and managers in the process is up to the individual agency, as long as they understand the advantages and the consequences of the decision.

## BEST PRACTICE

**Use this as an opportunity for political and career staff to learn from each other**—The tendency in identifying or selecting assessment participants is to think of this as a process that is most applicable and of most interest to career employees. However, politically appointed staff will have a different perspective on constituents and priorities. Involving both groups provides an opportunity for them to learn from each other.

## LANGUAGE

Even though it can create shared understanding, language also can be used to include or exclude groups of people, both employees and constituents, based on whether they can decode the meanings. It's important to remember that different groups have different ways of talking about work, and individuals and groups assign different words and meanings to workplace terminology. All too often, these differences become a barrier to sharing information between groups. Every organization has a language or vocabulary that its members use to describe the organization itself, its people, and its work processes both internally to staff members and externally to constituents and beneficiaries. This includes the commonly used terminology appropriate to the major profession or industry that they represent. Those in a transportation or public works department will use the language of engineering and planning. The staff of a commerce department will use the language of economics. This type of language also, without a doubt, includes its share of abbreviations, nicknames, and acronyms. *Getting Started* (Baldrige, 2003), a guidebook for conducting a self-assessment using the Baldrige program, lists "building a common language" as one of the principal reasons organizations initially undertake a self-assessment, saying "… you create opportunities for people across the organization to communicate with one another, perhaps for the first time. In effect, you are providing a common language so they can develop a common understanding of their organization's purpose, activities, and environment."[3]

## How to Prepare People for Participation

Once they are identified, it is important that the participants be given all the information and preparation necessary to ensure their success. Give some thought to the way in which people are notified about their participation, and emphasize that participants have been selected based on their institutional knowledge and perspective. For many people, it will be the first time that they have participated in this type of process, and it may require them to learn organizational development concepts and terminology, which are unfamiliar to them, including the meanings of the selected model and the specific categories of information to be considered. Using this framework, participants will discuss the organization as a larger system of interrelated functions. Rather than talking about individual offices, programs, or occupations, those who participate in an assessment are talking about leadership, planning, constituents, and other concepts that cut across all areas. All in all, it can be a different way of thinking and talking about the organization, as the process:

- encourages participants to describe work processes rather than work units
- calls for an answer to the question of what we mean when we talk about broad categories of work processes, such as information usage or what it means to consider workforce focus
- helps define what is considered organizational success, for example, not only what leadership is, but what it means to have effective leadership, and what the components are that go into evaluating it

Many organizations decide to conduct a training or orientation session for participants prior to an assessment process, which can be done using a facilitator who can be either internal or external to the agency, a training professional or the designated assessment process leader. Participants can learn about the assessment methodology to be used, which also provides them with a common language of assessment. The facilitator can educate participants on quality terminology and how these terms relate to the process by providing definitions and examples that will enable them to understand and apply the most important concepts.

This training, provided just prior to beginning the assessment, should

- explain the process to be used, including a review of the categories and the questions that will form the framework of the assessment
- introduce assessment and improvement terminology
- discuss the expectations of both management and the participants for the process and outcomes, including the amount of work, how the material will be presented, and the associated time frames
- identify the resources that will be available to the participants

Taking steps to prepare people in advance maximizes the time that they have available to spend working as a team once the assessment is underway.

## ORGANIZATIONAL IDENTIFICATION

Organizational identification can be defined as the way in which the individual views his or her personal connection to the agency. The strength of identification people have with their workplace varies, and the level can impact the way in which people make workplace decisions. Cheney (1983) believed that a person with a strong sense of organizational identification will evaluate choices and make decisions based on what he or she perceives to be in the best interests of the organization.

Higher levels of organizational identification also can be an outcome of the assessment process. Research has shown that the more interactions people have with others in the organization, the more likely it is that their identification with the organization will increase (Scott and Lane, 2000). Therefore, an organizational assessment can strengthen identification levels by facilitating interaction with staff from areas that they may not interact with on a day-to-day basis. An increase in identification with a group brings with it increased motivation to reach group goals rather than those that represent the self-interest of the individual (Scott and Lane, 2000). Therefore, a self-assessment process that increases organizational identification may be of value to the organization because it increases individual motivation toward the goals that are of importance to the organization.

## Endnotes

1. Weisbord (1987), p. 93.
2. An additional consideration in information collection is that while much of the information resides within the agency, some of it also may be external, residing with constituents, regulatory groups, legislators, or the community.
3. *Getting Started* (2003) National Institute of Standards and Technology, p. 10.

# Participant Demographics

This checklist contains a list of potential demographic categories for consideration. While they may not all be represented in your organization, use it as a guide to make sure that you have a good cross section of the agency participating. Place a check next to those demographic considerations that are represented. Supplement this list with representatives of the occupational disciplines that are most represented in your organization (i.e. engineers, social workers, human resources)

## 1. Job Category or Occupational Group

☐ Leaders

☐ Managers

☐ Professional

☐ Administrative

☐ Clerical

☐ Technical

☐ Specialists

## 2. Career Status

☐ Union

☐ Non-union

☐ Elected

☐ Appointed

☐ Career Service

## 3. Constituent Involvement

☐ Direct involvement with constituents

☐ Front-line service providers

☐ Internal service providers

## 4. Personal Demographics- Do participants reflect distribution based on:

☐ Gender

☐ Ethnicity

☐ Years of Service

☐ Education

Worksheet #12

# Chapter 5

# Conducting the Assessment

This chapter addresses the first two of the four stages of a structured assessment process: (1) creating a shared understanding of the current state of the organization and (2) identifying where the organization wants to be and what is needed to get there. It presents advice and checklists for implementing an assessment, including best practices. The model used in this chapter is the Public Sector Assessment and Improvement (PSAI) model, and the examples used will follow the categories and terminology of that model.

Tools include:

- Organizational Profile Worksheet
- PSAI Worksheets
- Approaches and Outcomes Worksheet (#13)
- Sample formats for workshops, project teams, and organization-wide teams

The planning is completed and the decisions have been made, the process manager and facilitator named, and the participants identified. Now begins the assessment itself. While the method selected will determine a large part of the actual work done, a structured assessment takes place in four stages:

Stage 1: Understanding the current state of the organization
Stage 2: Visioning and gap analysis
Stage 3: Improvement planning and prioritization
Stage 4: Outcomes and feedback

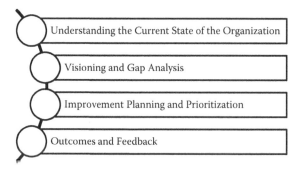

**Figure 5.1   The four stages of organizational assessment.**

The stages (Figure 5.1) are sequential, and the information generated at the conclusion of the process becomes part of the feedback used to restart the next cycle of assessment.

Organizations are complex structures, made up of many overlapping systems and processes. A structured assessment process provides a framework to locate and bring together data and information from across the organization, as well as information that may reside with other organizations or with the constituents and beneficiaries of its programs. It requires willingness to negotiate the meaning of the information so that agreement can be reached on a shared picture of the organization. The goal is to create an accurate picture of where the organization is now, where it would like to be, and the gaps that exist between those two points.

# Stage 1: Understanding the Current State of the Organization

The ability to conduct a thorough assessment of any government agency relies on three factors related to information and communication:

1. The existence of information about the organization, and its availability and accessibility
2. The willingness of the people who have access to that information to make it available in order to create a shared picture of the organization
3. The ability to analyze the information so that informed decisions about the state of the organization can be made

## Information Collection and Exchange

An organizational assessment begins with the collection of information and data from the organization that is to be the subject of the process, whether it's an entire agency or a smaller unit. The concept underlying this stage is to find a way to provide a common background to those who are studying the organization, so that everyone participating in the assessment has the same "picture" as a starting point. Because people may differ on how they see the organization, based on the information that may have been available to them in the past, this stage involves both collecting and exchanging information, and negotiating an agreement on what represents an accurate picture of the organization as it is now. They should ask:

- What would a profile of our organization include?
- What information do we have?
- What do we need to learn?
- What are the key values that define our organization?
- Who has the information that we need?
- How do we collect it?
- What information do we need from constituents?
- What are our trends?
- With whom should we compare ourselves?
- What is the most accurate picture of our current state?

The decision about what information will be collected is not random. The PSAI model, like other structured self-assessment processes, has a series of categories and an organizational profile outline, each of which contains a series of questions.

By answering those questions, participants construct a picture of the organization and the state of its activities. The collection and subsequent exchange of information needed to answer the questions in each assessment category constitute a communication process in which all participants share information to construct a more complete picture of the organization. Communication, which can be described as the exchange of information in order to create shared meaning, can be thought of as the engine that drives assessment, and the success of the assessment relies on the quality of the information that is exchanged. If the communication that takes place in an assessment is effective, it increases the likelihood that the process will result in meaningful outcomes.

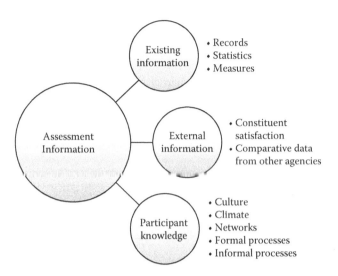

**Figure 5.2    Information sources for assessment processes.**

The process uses a combination of three types of information, as shown in Figure 5.2:

1. Information that already exists in the organization, such as records, statistics, written policies and procedures, and outcome measures
2. Information that can be collected or obtained from sources external to the organization, such as comparative data or benchmarks from similar organizations, and satisfaction levels of beneficiaries and constituents
3. Knowledge that exists within the members of the organization, such as an understanding of the culture, climate, networks, and formal and informal processes

The process of answering the questions that form the basis for the self-assessment incorporates two types of knowledge: personal knowledge and organizational knowledge. Personal knowledge is the information that participants have collected as a result of their own personal experiences in the organization. This can include communication, experiences, and perceptions, including interactions with co-workers, supervisors, and subordinates. It also can include experiences in dealing with constituents either first hand or by observing the way others manage their interactions. The information needed in order to respond to the questions may not be readily available or known to the participants. The nature of the questions requires participants to reach outside their personal knowledge to other sources inside and outside the organization to gather information and data with which they may not be familiar.

Organizational knowledge can be defined as data and information about the organization itself: processes, policies, procedures, and structure.

## BEST PRACTICES

**Communicate progress**—Throughout the process, communicate the progress being made to the rest of the employees. This is especially important if team-based processes are being used where people may contribute information, but not see results for some time. Communication can include, where appropriate, newsletters or other bulletins outlining progress to date and expected completion dates.

## *Information Collection: The Organizational Profile*

The first step in structured assessment processes is to create an organizational profile, which is a brief overview of basic information describing the agency, including its purpose or mission and basic structural and demographic information. It may, at first thought, seem superfluous to have the agency members develop a profile of their own agency, but many times people only have limited knowledge of the organizational structure and demographics, or understand only their part of the organization without knowing how the pieces fit together. The idea is to capture as broad a description as possible, and to use it as a framework or context for how the information in the assessment can be understood. The organizational profile can be developed by the participants as a whole, or alternatively, it can be prepared by an individual or team and presented to the group as part of their resource material. The **PSAI Organizational Profile Checklist** (page 107) provides a list of questions to guide development of the profile.

The answers should include enough detail to create a thorough picture. For example, a description of the governance structure could, in local government, include the administrative management as well as the elected or appointed officials. Boards and commissions that are part of larger state agencies would describe how they are linked and the required approval structure, for example, if the minutes of board meetings must be approved by the governor in order to be official. Organizational location or points of service should include all regularly used locations. In a parks and recreational department this could include a list of all the neighborhood parks and facilities available in which staff members are located or conduct programs. In a public works or transportation agency, it could include all the district or regional maintenance headquarters and yards. At the federal level, it could include regional or state-based offices.

## Information Collection: The Assessment Categories

The most extensive part of the information collection process supplies the qualitative and quantitative information about how the organization functions and the outcomes that are achieved relative to its goals. Much of the information developed in the information-gathering parts of an assessment process is qualitative; that is, it includes not only factual information or data about the organization, but people's reaction, feelings, impressions, and descriptions. It considers the organizational culture and the workforce climate. This qualitative information is very much a part of understanding how the organization functions and is very useful in determining the impact of all the information collected. However, it must be balanced by the use of quantitative, verifiable information to facilitate the comparison and prioritization of opportunities for improvement. This can include *benchmarking*, which is obtaining comparative information about other organizations with similar processes.

### BEST PRACTICES

**Select appropriate benchmarking partners**—Part of the process of information gathering is the identification of appropriate benchmarking targets; that is, the organizations within or outside government that will be used for comparisons. Folz (2004) conducted a study of benchmarking in municipalities, in which he concludes that successful benchmarking requires not only the selection of comparable organizations, but that the likelihood of success can be improved if the organizations selected for benchmarking are performing at the level that the organization wishes to achieve and which the constituents are willing to support. He suggests that it is important to focus not just on the highest performers, but those with comparable citizen expectations. Folz says that the community's challenge is to find "benchmarking partners that provide the service at the desired level of quality and to identify the best practices that explain why that partner is able to provide the service at a higher level of efficiency and effectiveness" (p. 211).

The PSAI model consists of seven categories (see Appendix A for a more detailed explanation of the categories). The categories representing leadership, constituents, and the workforce are referred to as the Human Factors group because they address the ways in which individuals think, act, communicate, and influence others in order to shape the behavior of the organization. Factors in this area are affected by interpersonal relations, communication competency, and emotional intelligence:

■ The **Leadership** category addresses leadership structure, practices, and ethics. It covers the actions of leaders in directing the day-to-day and long-term operations of the agency, maintaining a clear focus on the mission, supporting the workforce in accomplishing their goals, and establishing ways to incorporate and address the needs and expectations of the constituents and beneficiaries that they serve. Leaders make decisions and enact policies that influence the perceptions of employees on their mission, vision, values, and services. This directly impacts the way that the members of the workforce view their responsibilities toward the jurisdiction and the constituents that they serve.

■ The **Workforce** category focuses on the agency's most valuable resource—its people. It considers how the agency manages, supports, and develops the workforce so that they can use their full potential to support the mission, vision, and plans. Excellence in the public sector depends on the ability of staff members to deliver services in a competent, effective, and efficient way. It relies on staff knowledge and expertise, combined with the ability and desire to work collectively for the public good. Therefore, it is important to create an organizational culture that encourages high-quality practices, and which both enables and motivates people to achieve high-performance levels. The organization has to build and maintain a climate that values excellence, diversity, collaboration, learning, and personal and professional development. Just as important, workplaces must provide environmentally safe work locations and practices as well as workplaces that safeguard the security of the workforce.

■ **Constituents** make up the third part of this triad, and their interaction with the workforce drives decisions about effectiveness. This category looks at how the agency identifies the needs, expectations, perspectives, and satisfaction level of the agency's constituents: the individuals, groups, publics, and organizations for which you provide programs or services. It considers the way the agency identifies and builds relationships with constituents and how it determines their needs, expectations, and satisfaction levels.

The second set of three categories is called the Operational Factors group, and includes the categories of strategic planning, measurement and analysis, and programs and processes. This group addresses the way in which the organization carries out its operations. The factors in this group are impacted by—and rely on—information, process documentation, and shared data:

- **Strategic planning** is comprised of the goals, objectives, and activities needed to direct the work of the agency. This category looks at the manner in which the mission is translated into a set of goals, and how the agency develops and implements short- and long-term plans and strategies to advance those goals. It also reviews how these plans and goals are disseminated throughout the organization, and how progress on plans and goals is assessed. In addition to goals and plans, this category also looks at the values of the organization, which might be defined as the attributes that employees can expect from their co-workers as they perform their jobs.
- **Programs and processes** are the actions through which the work is carried out. The emphasis in this category is on how these programs are designed, and how their corresponding processes are standardized, documented, monitored, and continually improved to achieve the highest possible levels of effectiveness and efficiency and to meet the needs and expectations of the groups being served.
- **Measurement and analysis** drives strategic planning and provides a way of monitoring its effectiveness. This category examines how the agency shares and utilizes information, knowledge, and expertise internally and externally. The question becomes what and how much information to share to convey a sense of the current status without overwhelming people with data that is so extensive as to be meaningless. Many organizations identify a small set of core measures that are vital to accomplishing the mission of the organization or key to identifying and communicating the success of a particular program.

The constant interaction of the two groups enables the organization to function. Those on the Human Factors side of the equation continually make decisions or take actions that impact the Operational Factors, which in turn influence the decisions and actions of leaders, staff, and constituents. Bridging these two groups is the seventh category: **Outcomes**. This category represents the collective performance measurement outcomes that signify the results of the ways that the other six areas perform.

The PSAI worksheets (page 107) provide the questions to be used in collecting the information needed for the assessment in each of the seven categories. The answers to these questions, which highlight the key facets of each category, provide the core information needed to examine the organization and form the basis for identifying strengths and opportunities for improvement. It's important to note that the organization is not limited to these questions. If desired, the list of questions can be supplemented to capture any areas of particular interest or unique facets of the organization.

## How Is the Information Collected?

The questions can be used as part of any method of assessment. For example, the questions can be put into a survey format and distributed across the organization.[1] The results then can be compiled for use. The answers can be collected in a workshop, by asking the participants, as a whole or in subgroups, to provide the information that they have available to them. The questions can be assigned to project teams or organization-wide teams for investigation, which, because it is not limited to what people know and can articulate in a single session, allows more in-depth information collection efforts. Sample formats for workshop and team assessments are provided at the end of this chapter. (Conducting a PSAI Assessment Workshop, Managing a PSAI Workshop using a Project Team, Managing a PSAI Assessment using an Organization-Wide Team.)

Once this information has been collected and brought to the table (literally and figuratively), the participants in the assessment process pool the information to create a picture of the organization. Because assessment is a fact-based process, the information that is finally incorporated into the assessment must ultimately be objective and verifiable rather than simply anecdotal. The usability of the outcomes from the assessment depends in large part on the quality of the information collected during the process.

## Negotiation and Consensus Building

Even though they participate in the information collection, people may still disagree about the validity and relative importance of some of the information being exchanged. As a result, participants use two related communication processes—negotiation and consensus—to resolve the differences in their perceptions and reach agreement on the strengths and opportunities. Everett Rogers (1995), in his work on the diffusion of innovation in organizations, describes communication as:

> "   a process in which participants create and share information with one another in order to reach a mutual understanding. This definition implies that communication is a process of convergence (or divergence) as two or more individuals exchange information in order to move toward each other (or apart) in the meanings that they give to certain events."[2]

Once the information needed to answer the category questions has been collected, it is important to make sure that it is not only shared with others, but that there is agreement on what the information means and represents. This is accomplished by negotiating a common interpretation. Negotiation, in the context of organizational assessment, is a communication process in which people discuss the differences in their perceptions of information and its meaning in order to come to a consensus, or a common, agreed upon definition of what the information represents.

People can consider the same information, but assign different meanings to it. The negotiation process provides a way to compare the information that has been collected and pooled in order to reach agreement on a picture or collective understanding of the agency. The goal is to reach a consensus on a shared view of the organization and its needs. Applying Rogers' definition to the assessment process, the purpose is to use communication to foster convergence about the information and what it means.

The diagram in Figure 5.3 shows how this negotiation process takes place.

The individual participants contribute the information they have collected (based on their personal knowledge combined with other data to which they have access) to create a pool of information. Within that pool, there may be information and descriptions that do not match. The information contributed by Participant 1 and the information contributed by Participant 2 may represent different perspectives on a process, or the relationship between units. As they discuss the information, they negotiate a shared meaning. For example, in an assessment process that took

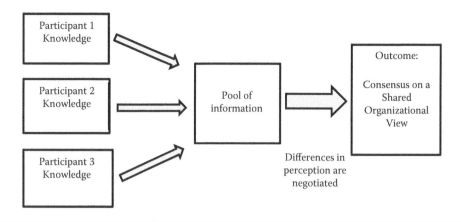

**Figure 5.3   Negotiation in the organizational assessment process.**

place in a state agency, the following conversation occurred. It concerned constituent information, and whether the staff received any feedback from constituents.

*Participant A:* We don't get any complaints from people.
*Participant B:* Are you kidding? Am I the only one who sees the complaints come in? I open the letters, and people do have complaints sometimes.
*Participant A:* Well, I never see those letters.
*Participant C:* Maybe we need to have a process so that people know when a complaint or question comes in.

   If you had asked the participants prior to this exchange whether they ever receive critical feedback from constituents, Participants A and C would have said "no," and Participant B would have said "yes." From each of their individual perspectives, their answer would have been accurate. The difference is that only Participant B had access to the information about constituent feedback. This brief conversation was, in fact, a negotiation. Participant A presented his or her information. Participant B countered with different information. The result of this negotiation/discussion was a shared understanding among the participants that their unit, in fact, did receive complaints from constituents, but also that this information was not being made available to staff. In this case, the negotiation also directly contributed to a recommendation for improvement—the creation of a feedback process.
   The negotiation process also encourages the development of systems thinking among the participants. The process of presenting and comparing

### BEST PRACTICE

**Capture organizational stories**—Look for opportunities throughout the process to listen to and capture organizational "stories." Are there stories that people tell that describe the essence of what the organization is all about? These can be positive stories about, for example, how employees felt they were supported on an important issue, or how the organization celebrated a big success. They can also be negative stories, which describe behaviors or values that are not considered part of the organization's culture. Such stories can be used both in the assessment process and outside of it to build organizational identification and to solidify the organizational identity.

information to identify the degree to which there is agreement and the degree to which differences exist and must be resolved is intended to get people out of their organizational silos and create a picture of how all the various pieces fit together in a system. They learn how the parts of the organization interact to accomplish the work, where links exist and where they might be missing. W. Edwards Deming (American statistician and author often referred to as the Father of the quality movement) speaks of the potential of cross-functional teams, such as those often used in assessment processes, to "break down barriers between departments."[3]

### BEST PRACTICE

**Create an environment where there is a willingness to challenge information**—An important part of the assessment process is to bring together information from various sources and perspectives, which means that not all the information will line up; in other words, there will be different interpretations based on the workforce experiences of the participants. The assessment process needs to allow people to challenge information and beliefs that they believe are not accurate or do not correctly explain the workings of the agency, so that they can reach agreement on the best possible explanation. In order to create a realistic awareness of the strengths and opportunities for improvement, participants must feel that challenging information is not only appropriate, but welcomed.

# Stage 2: Visioning and Gap Analysis

One of the major goals of assessment is to determine what changes are needed to improve the agency's effectiveness, its efficiency, and its overall ability to fulfill its mission and appropriately serve its constituents. Not only does the process result in the collection of information, it provides a mechanism for identifying the gaps between an agency's current ability to provide these programs and services and the level of performance needed to fully achieve its mission. This stage, Visioning and Gap Analysis, calls for an analysis of the agency based on the knowledge created in the information collection and exchange. Ideally, organizational leaders have identified their vision for the agency or program, and can communicate this to the assessment leader and the participants. The vision might take the form of increased efficiency and effectiveness in meeting the agency's existing mission or it may include future goals that differ from those that currently exist. The vision provides the comparison point that allows assessment participants to identify the gap between where the organization is now and where it feels it should be.

- What are our strengths?
- What are our opportunities for improvement?
- How strong are we in each category?

## WHAT SHOULD WE BE DOING?

Assessment asks not only whether the measures or results are good or bad, strong or weak, positive or negative, but whether the combination of processes, programs, and people used to achieve the results are operating in a way that will produce the best possible outcomes. Taking this one step farther, it asks whether the programs and processes should be done at all, and opens an opportunity to talk about eliminating programs that don't further the organizational mission. The authors of the budget language that introduced the federal Performance Assessment Rating Tool recognized that measuring performance was not enough; that a program could be very effective and yet not be an appropriate role for government. President Clinton's stated purpose in enacting the Government Performance and Results Act was to use performance information to ask not only whether government was doing well, but whether it was doing the right things: "We know we have to go beyond cutting, even beyond restructuring, to completely reevaluate what the federal government is doing. Are we doing it well? Should we be doing it at all? Should someone else be doing it?"[4]

## Identifying Strengths and Opportunities for Improvement

Once the information collected by the participants is exchanged and a shared organizational view has been negotiated, the next step is to compare it to the vision and determine what it would take to achieve that level of operation and performance. A two-part gap analysis is accomplished by mining the information developed in Stage 1.

In the first part of the gap analysis process, participants review the information in each category and identify those things that they believe represent the strengths of the agency and those things that must be improved in order to close the gap between the present and the desired state. Given the sheer volume of information that can be developed in the earlier information-gathering stages, identifying these factors can be a challenging process. Participants can identify common themes as well as specific bottlenecks or problems, and present them as individual statements. Statements that are clear, specific, and understandable by participants and nonparticipants alike will have the greatest chance of influencing action. The result will be two lists for each of the PSAI categories: one that lists the strengths, and one that lists the opportunities for improvement.

There is a commonly used expression that "where you stand depends on where you sit" and it certainly applies to the effort to extract these strengths and opportunities. Depending on his or her position and role in the organization, one participant might see certain information as a current strength while another participant with a different organizational perspective believes that it requires improvement. For example, take the case of the discussion on constituent feedback above in Negotiation and Consensus Building, in which participants disagreed about whether people were happy with their services. In that example, one set of participants believed that constituents were happy, because they didn't receive any complaints, only to be told by the administrative staff that they most certainly received complaints, but didn't share them. The first step of the gap analysis might produce the following results, which would be listed in the constituent category:

Strength:

■ Constituents provide feedback on projects by mail and electronic correspondence.

Opportunities for improvement:

■ There is no process for sharing constituent feedback with those working on the projects.
■ There is no formal policy or process for responding to constituent feedback.
■ Constituent feedback is not recorded in any systematic way.

Opportunities for improvement resulting from this situation also might be captured in other categories.

Programs and Processes Category:

■ Constituent feedback is not used in evaluating the outcomes of projects.
■ There is no process for reviewing constituent feedback in order to improve processes.

Workforce Category:

■ Constituent feedback is not considered when giving performance feedback to staff members.

Each perspective is a bit different, and helps highlight the opportunity for multiple improvements.

One of the benefits of the assessment process is that all the participants are working from the same set of information. Hutton (2000) in his research on consensus building, suggests that when people are being presented with the same set of information, they become more likely to reach similar conclusions about the current state of the organization, and what it needs to move forward.

The second stage of the gap analysis process asks participants to evaluate the information collected in each category using three criteria:

1. To what extent does the organization have a positive approach; that is, does it have effective, documented practices and positive outcomes to all the issues covered by the questions contained in this category?
2. Does a positive approach to this category exist in all areas of the organization, some areas, or not at all?
3. Does the available data indicate that the organization is improving over time in each of the categories?

The Approaches and Outcomes Worksheet (#13) can be used to complete this part of the gap analysis. By determining the answers to those three questions, a comparison of the relative strength of the agency in each category can be made. For example, Agency A may have a systematic approach to strategic planning that is in place across the organization. They are recognized as a leader in this area; in fact, the governor has asked them to present their approach to the rest of the Cabinet officers. Using the Approaches and Outcomes Worksheet, they would be rated "Excellent" in the Strategic Planning category. However, Agency A does not have a similar approach to their programs and processes. A few divisions have documented their core processes, but the practice is not widespread. They have just started to benchmark against other agencies. Using

### BEST PRACTICE

**Don't lose sight of the positive**—It's easy for an assessment process to become a complaint session for everything that's wrong. Instead of focusing on the opportunities, it's also easy to turn this into an analysis of "why we are the way we are." An example could be the tendency of some people to focus on the dysfunctional leader who left years ago. It's important to remind them that the history cannot be undone, but the process can accomplish the most by focusing on the positive to move forward. Incorporate the concept of appreciative inquiry, an approach to evaluation and assessment that asks people to focus on instances where the organization has performed especially well, and identify the factors that made it work so successfully.

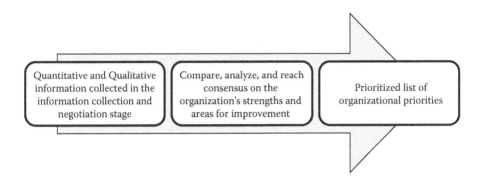

**Figure 5.4 The information collected in the assessment is mined for organizational strengths and opportunities for improvement. In the same way that participants negotiated agreement on the information, they negotiate agreement on the organization's strengths and areas for improvement. This provides the foundation for the next stage, where the relative priorities of those opportunities are determined.**

the Approaches and Outcomes Worksheet, they would be rated "Fair" in the Programs and Processes category. Understanding the relative strength of the agency in each category can be a useful tool in setting priorities for further action (Figure 5.4).

# Endnotes

1. A survey can be used both as an assessment method and as a tool for use by a project team or organization-wide team.
2. Rogers (1995), pp. 5–6.
3. Cornin (2004), p. 46.
4. Gore (1995), p. 37.

# PSAI Organizational Profile Worksheet

## A. Organizational Purpose

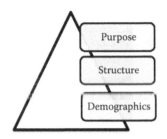

- What is the mission of the organization? What is the enabling legislation that establishes the organization and its purposes? What changes have been made to that legislation to expand or change those original purposes and responsibilities?
- What jurisdiction does this organization represent? What are the demographic features of the jurisdiction?

## B. Structure

- How is the agency organized? Describe the structure including the levels of the organization, its divisions or subunits, and its links to other agencies, such as commissions or boards that may fall under its jurisdiction.
- What is the management structure?
- What is the governance structure? Are there other levels of government to which this organization reports? What are they, and what are the primary points of contact? What degree of autonomy exists between these levels of government?
- Where is the organization located, including its primary location or headquarters and other major facilities including regional locations and points of service?

## C. Demographics

- How many employees are in this organization? How has this number changed over time? What are the critical demographic features?

- What are the major job categories and the number of people currently assigned to each?
- What are the primary professions represented?
- Who are the labor representatives, and what groups do they represent?

# Public Sector Assessment and Improvement Worksheets

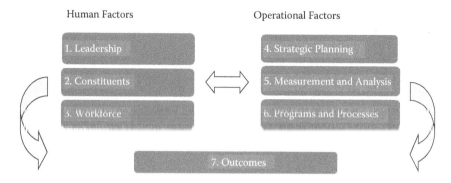

## *Human Factors*

## *Category 1: Leadership*

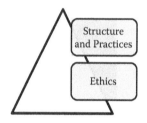

A. Leadership Structure and Practices

- What is the leadership structure? Who is included when we talk about leaders?
- What actions do leaders take to communicate and build a commitment to the mission across the organization?
- What steps do leaders take to define their priorities and make sure they are clear and understood across the organization?
- How do leaders review and monitor performance and progress on plans and goals?
- How do leaders promote a focus on the needs of beneficiaries and constituents—the people for whom you provide services?
- How do senior leaders build public and legislative support for the organization's priorities and plans? How successful are those efforts?
- In what ways are leaders visible to and accessible to employees?
- What steps do leaders take to advocate for the agency and its needs?

■ How do leaders at all levels of the organization share their expertise and experience with the organization?

3. Ethical Leadership

■ What do leaders do to emphasize the importance of integrity and ethical behavior across the agency?
■ What actions do leaders take to demonstrate their personal integrity and to promote ethical behavior? How do they model ethical behavior?
■ What are the areas of potential ethical concern for the organization (such as conflicts of interest, bidding processes, nepotism, or inappropriate influence)? What mechanisms are in place to address each of these areas?
■ What impact do the agency's operations have on the community in which it is located? What impact does it have on the environment? How are these addressed in a proactive manner?
■ What are the legal and regulatory requirements that pertain to the organization's operations, and how are these requirements and associated standards met? How is this information made known throughout the organization?

## Category 2: Constituents

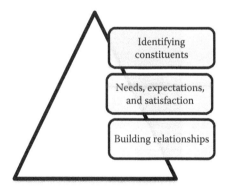

A. Identifying Constituents

■ Who are the major constituent groups that benefit from the work of the organization?

■ What are the primary programs and services provided to each group?

■ What other constituent groups have an interest in the services provided, even if they are not direct beneficiaries?

■ How are these groups changing? What constituent groups have been added or are anticipated to change in the next two years?

B. Assessing Constituent Needs, Expectations, and Satisfaction

■ What information is collected on a regular basis about the needs and priorities of each of these groups? How is it collected, and how often is it collected?

■ How is this information used to anticipate future needs?

■ How do you determine current satisfaction levels of individuals, groups, and organizations with the services provided?

■ What are the most critical needs and expectations of each constituent group?

■ What changes are anticipated in the critical needs and expectations of these groups over the next one to five years?

■ How, and to what degree, does the organization seek diversity in the participation of constituents, i.e., drawing participation from many groups who may have different viewpoints, rather than only those who share the same policy perspective?

C. Building Constituent Relationships

■ What actions are taken to include constituent needs, expectations, perspectives, and satisfaction levels in project planning?

■ How do you incorporate this information in performance measures and standards, such as standards regarding waiting times, telephone callback response time and responding to letters of complaint, or in terms of expectations for service?

■ How is information about programs and services in general, and about specific projects made available to constituents? (For example, public forums, newsletters, Web sites.)

■ What staff groups have regular and significant contact with members of constituent groups? How does this contact take place, and how is the quality of the interaction monitored?

- What steps are taken to ensure that people have access to programs and/or services at times and places that are convenient and appropriate to their needs?
- What methods are used to identify and assist people who need special assistance or accommodations to enable them to use the agency's services?
- What processes are in place for people to provide feedback about programs and services?

## Category 3: Workforce Focus

A. Workforce Planning

- What process is used to identify current and future workforce needs? How frequently are anticipated workforce needs reviewed?
- What are the critical jobs in your organization without which the work of the organization could not be done?
- What functions if any are currently outsourced?
- What are the core competencies and skills for each major employee group or job category? What steps are taken to anticipate new skills that will be needed in the future?
- How are current skill sets and competencies assessed?
- What processes are in place to ensure that new employees are recruited in a manner that recognizes and supports diversity?
- What formal processes are in place to address succession planning and retention of organizational knowledge?
- Are career development processes in place, including career counseling and mentoring? How accessible are these processes to the workforce as a whole?

- How are collaborative work practices, including cross-training, cross-organizational teams, and task forces, used to increase employee knowledge and abilities?
- How is demographic information tracked and used in workforce planning?

B. Performance Assessment and Recognition

- What systems are in place to review performance review and provide feedback? How do these systems encourage outstanding performance?
- Do performance review systems encourage excellence in both individual performance and excellence in team performance and collaboration?
- How are individual and team excellence recognized and reinforced?

C. Learning and Professional Development

- How are new knowledge, skills, and capabilities needed by staff identified?
- What methods (for example, classroom, online, Web casts, subject matter experts, on-the-job training, contracted training or tuition reimbursement) are used to make training and professional development available and accessible to employees?
- What standards or goals exist for ensuring the amount of training made available to all employees?
- How are professional development programs evaluated?
- What are the major subject areas or categories of training and professional development available to staff?

D. Workplace Climate

- What processes are in place to assess and improve workplace health, safety, and ergonomics?
- What procedures are in place to ensure a secure workplace where employees will be free from harm?
- How does the agency ensure that the workplace is free from discrimination and harassment?
- How does the agency ensure that the workplace is prepared for emergencies, natural, health, or environmental disasters and security emergencies? What plans exist, and how are they communicated to staff and reinforced?

- What is the relationship between organizational leaders and employee representatives, such as unions or associations? How are communications between the organization and these groups maintained?
- What methods (such as surveys, interviews, exit interviews, or measures of staff retention, absenteeism, and productivity) are used to assess the workplace climate and staff satisfaction levels? How and how often is this satisfaction and climate information gathered?

## Operational Factors

### Category 4: Strategic Planning

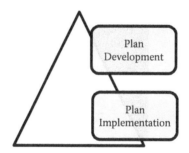

A. Strategic Plan Development

- Is there a formal, adopted statement of the organization's mission and vision?
- To what extent is the mission defined by law or regulation? What are the applicable laws and regulations, and how is this information made known to employees?
- Has the organization identified its core values and communicated them to employees?
- How does the organization translate the mission and vision into plans and goals?
- Is there a formal, documented strategic planning process? If so, what are the major steps in the process? Does it take place on a regularly scheduled basis?
- Does the planning process include an analysis of the current environment (strengths, weaknesses, opportunities, and threats) as well as information from any previous organizational assessments, self-studies, internal and/or external audits or reviews?

- How are staff members involved in the planning process? How is staff input and feedback encouraged and incorporated in the planning process?
- How are goals, strategies, and action plans determined for all levels of the organization?
- How does the planning process incorporate information about:
  - Trends in the jurisdiction (for example, the city, district, county, or state)?
  - Funding issues and resources (both current and anticipated)?
  - Legislative environment and pending or proposed legislation?
  - Organizational capabilities?
  - Information on needs and expectations of constituents?
  - Human, fiscal, and other resources needed to accomplish the mission?
- How does the planning process align human and fiscal resources with identified goals?
- How are goals, strategies, and action steps established?
- What actions are taken to ensure that plans throughout the organization are aligned with the larger organizational goals and plans?

B. Implementing the Strategic Plan

- What steps are taken to communicate the plan to all employees, and to build commitment for the plan throughout the organization?
- What steps are taken to ensure that people have a clear understanding of the goals, strategies, and actions to be taken?
- How is the plan implemented? Who is responsible for its implementation?
- How is progress toward goals, objectives, strategies, and actions monitored?
- What processes are in place to adapt the plan for changes in available fiscal and human resources, organizational capabilities, and unantici- pated obstacles, challenges, and opportunities?
- What performance measures or key performance indicators are used to measure progress toward goals, strategies, and action plans?
- What steps are taken to ensure that organizational decision making at all levels is guided by the strategic plan?

# Category 5: Measurement and Analysis

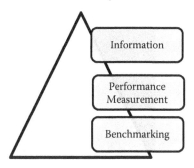

## A. Information

- What information is collected about major work programs and processes?
- How is information collected and disseminated so it is available for use?
- What information is required by regulatory or other external agencies?
- Are information systems user-friendly?
- What actions are taken to ensure the integrity, reliability, accuracy, timeliness, and security of data and information?
- What safeguards are in place to protect data security and employee/constituent privacy considerations?

## B. Performance Measurement

- What performance measures are used to determine the organization's performance against the mission, plans, and goals?
- How are performance measures or indicators developed?
- How are performance indicators reported throughout your organization?
- How does the agency review performance measures to make sure that they reflect current priorities?

## C. Benchmarking

- How does the agency use data and information to compare current outcomes and measures with the outcomes from previous years?

■ How does the agency compare its information with that of other organizations to evaluate outcomes and achievements? What organizations are currently used for benchmarking, and why were they selected? Do the organizations chosen reflect government agencies at the same or other levels of government, and/or those in other sectors?

## Category 6: Programs and Processes

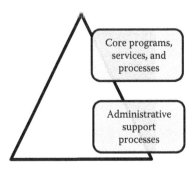

A. Core Programs, Services, and Processes

■ What are the organization's core programs and services?
■ What are the major processes associated with each core program or service?
■ What constituent groups are served by each program or service?
■ How are new programs or services developed?
■ What steps are taken to ensure that core processes are appropriately standardized, documented, and monitored?
■ How do you ensure that new and existing processes make the best use of available technology?
■ What performance measures or indicators are used to assess the effectiveness and efficiency of core processes?
■ How often are core processes reviewed and (if needed) redesigned?

B. Administrative Support Processes

■ What are the organization's most important administrative support processes?
■ What steps are taken to ensure that administrative support processes are appropriately standardized, documented, and monitored?

- How do you ensure that new and existing administrative support processes make the best use of available technology?
- What performance measures or indicators are used to assess the effectiveness and efficiency of administrative support processes?
- How often are support processes reviewed and (if needed) redesigned?

## Category 7: Results

A. Performance Measures and Results
   For each of the other six categories:

- What are the results associated with each measure of organizational performance?
- How do these outcomes compare to information from the previous year(s)?
- How do these outcomes compare to those of other, similar organizations?
- How do these outcomes compare to established targets or goals?

# Approaches and Outcomes Worksheet

| Rating | Approach/Implementation/Outcomes |
|---|---|
| **Excellent** | All areas of the category are addressed<br>A systematic approach to assessment and improvement is in place in all parts of the organization<br>There is a pattern of excellent performance results over time<br>Recognized as a government leader in the category |
| **Vory Good** | Most of the areas of the category are addressed<br>A systematic approach to assessment and improvement is in place throughout most of the organization<br>There is a pattern of very good outcomes and positive trends which compare favorably to other organizations<br>Recognized as a government leader in some aspects of the category |
| **Good** | Many of the areas of the category are addressed<br>A systematic approach to assessment and improvement is in place in many areas, although there are some gaps<br>There is a pattern of good to very good current outcomes, including good comparisons to other organizations |
| **Fair** | Some of the areas of the category are addressed<br>A systematic approach to assessment and improvement is in place in some areas, although there are major gaps<br>There are positive current outcomes, and the beginning of a program to track trends or benchmark other organizations |
| **Preliminary** | Few of the areas of this category are addressed, or the category criteria are addressed in only a few programs, services, or processes<br>The beginning of a systematic approach to assessing and improving **effectiveness and efficiency in some areas**<br>Some positive outcomes, but little or no comparisons to others |
| **No positive approach** | No systematic approach to category<br>Only anecdotal information on approach and implementation<br>No documented results<br>No documented comparisons |

Using the descriptions in the table, assess the approach, performance, and outcomes in each category to determine the extent to which effective, documented practices and positive outcomes exist throughout the organization. For each category, enter the description which best matches the current state of the agency or area undergoing assessment:

| Category | Rating |
|---|---|
| Leadership | |
| Constituents | |
| Workforce | |
| Strategic Planning | |
| Measurement and Analysis | |
| Programs and Processes | |

**Worksheet #13**

# Conducting a PSAI Assessment Workshop

Participants: Selected organizational members, process leaders or assessment facilitator, organizational leader
Time frame: 1 or 2 days

Agenda

- Explanation of assessment purpose by an organizational leader
- Description of process by the process leader/assessment facilitator
- For each category, participants:
  - Review the PSAI Worksheet for one category at a time. Discuss the
    questions assigned to that category. Present, exchange and record
    information needed to answer the questions, including examples,
    organizational stories, and participant perceptions.
  - Review the information collected; negotiate any differences in per-
    ceptions until there is a shared understanding/organizational view.
- Analyze the information collected for each category:
  - Identify, reach consensus on, and record the organization's strengths
  - Identify, reach consensus on and record the opportunities for
    improvement
- Evaluate and reach consensus on the organization's approach to
  each category

The deliverable at the end of the workshop will be an unranked or unpri-
oritized list of opportunities for improvement.

# Managing a PSAI Assessment Using a Project Team

Participants: Process leader and/or assessment facilitator, identified project team members

Initial Meeting Agenda:

- Explanation of assessment purpose by an organizational leader
- Description of process by the process leader/assessment facilitator
- Review questions for each category
- Develop a schedule of future meetings (weekly, monthly)

Process

- Prior to the next meeting, team members use all available sources, including co-workers, supervisors, managers, organizational leaders, documents (written and electronic), policies and procedures, and organizational stories to find the information needed to answer the category questions.
- At subsequent meetings:
  - For each PSAI category, discuss the questions assigned to that category. Present the information collected by team members. (If the group chooses, information can be submitted and compiled prior to the meeting.)
  - Discuss the information; negotiate any differences in perceptions until there is a shared understanding/organizational view.
  - Analyze the information collected:
    - Identify and record the organization's strengths in each category
    - Identify and record the opportunities for improvement in each category
- Evaluate and reach consensus on the organization's approach to each category

# Managing a PSAI Assessment Using an Organization-Wide Team

Participants: Process leader and/or assessment facilitator, identified
team members

Initial Meeting Agenda:

- Explanation of assessment purpose by an organizational leader
- Description of process by the process leader/assessment facilitator
- Review questions for each category
- Divide participants into subteams. Assign a category to each subteam;
  a subteam can be responsible for the questions pertaining to their
  assigned category, and also for the outcome information for that cat-
  egory requested in Category 7
- Develop a schedule of future meetings (weekly, monthly)

Process

- Prior to the next meeting, subteam members use all available sources,
  including co-workers, supervisors, managers, organizational leaders, documents (written and electronic), policies and procedures, and organizational stories to find the information needed to answer the questions for
  their assigned category, including the outcome information for Category 7:
  - For each PSAI category, discuss the questions assigned to that cat-
    egory. Discuss the information; negotiate any differences in percep-
    tions until there is a shared understanding/organizational view.
  - Analyze the information collected:
    - Identify and record the organization's strengths in each category
    - Identify and record the opportunities for improvement in each
      category
    - Evaluate and reach consensus on the organization's approach to
      each category
- At subsequent meetings:
  - Subteam members present a summary of the information found for
    that category, and the strengths and opportunities for improvement
    they have identified.
- The process leader compiles the reports from each subteam.

# Chapter 6

# Linking Assessment and Improvement

This concluding chapter discusses the way in which assessment is linked to planning and improvement, as the outcomes of the assessment process are communicated to the organization as a whole and the improvement plans are implemented. It describes ways to create a culture of assessment through periodic assessment processes and summarizes the key success factors in sustaining organizational assessment.

You have conducted an organizational assessment and have, as a result, a list of strengths and opportunities for improvement, and a sense of the relative strengths of the organization in each of the assessment categories. To ensure the success of the efforts, and make it more than just an information-gathering exercise, it is critical that those involved follow through on the work that's been accomplished. While an organizational assessment process can be a powerful tool for identifying the current state of the agency and creating an awareness of what is possible, awareness itself does not move the organization forward.

The full benefit lies in completing the cycle of assessment and improvement by using the information obtained to initiate and bring about improvement consistent with the mission and vision of the organization. Without a doubt, an agency that has completed an assessment process and identified opportunities for improvement has accomplished a great deal, and gained many benefits in terms of employee communication and personal/organizational learning, but if few (or none) of the resulting recommendations for improvement are implemented, participants and observers alike will be frustrated, making it that much more difficult for leaders and employees to justify participation in the future. This is where the remaining two stages of organizational assessment take place.

## Stage 3: Improvement Planning and Prioritization

This stage in the assessment process looks at how the information learned during the assessment can be put to work to initiate changes. It encompasses several critical components:

■ Prioritizing opportunities for improvement
■ Identifying projects
■ Action planning
■ Implementing the improvement priorities

Taken together, these actions make the assessment more than just a document or report, and provide evidence of tangible results. It makes the assessment process "real" for both those who participated and those who were aware that the process was taking place, but did not have the opportunity to be part of it. To be successful, all of this must be done while considering the dynamics of change and the role of change management.

What are our priorities for change?
What can we reasonably do?
What resources will it require?
What will we do?
Who will be responsible?
How will we measure our accomplishments?

The knowledge developed during an assessment can establish the groundwork for change by providing the supporting information on which decisions can be made. Why is this so critical? Just as failure to enact any recommendations will damage the credibility of the assessment effort, trying to enact too many changes at once, or unsupported changes, can have the same outcome. Initiating change without a firm understanding of an organization's current capabilities and resources can result in false starts and wasted resources, and jeopardize support for change in the future.

### BEST PRACTICE

**Create realistic expectations**—It's important to be aware of the expectations that introducing an assessment process creates. One of the issues in any kind of organizational intervention, not just assessment processes, is that it creates an expectation that things are going to change. Assessment leaders must be careful not to lead people to think that every opportunity for improvement will be accomplished or even that every improvement plan will be completely followed out. They must communicate in a way that is realistic about the amount of change that can take place. For example, an agency may be located in a less than adequate facility, and it's reasonable to assume that one of the "opportunities" that participants will identify is to relocate to another building. Unfortunately, the control of building leases may rest with another agency, and it may not be possible to make a change for a long time, or not at all. Be clear that an assessment process does not change the fact that certain factors are outside the control of the agency, and look for opportunities that you can control.

## Prioritizing Opportunities and Identifying Projects

Once the process has helped determine what improvements are possible, the prioritization and project planning stages help set a path for determining what will be done and how the necessary changes can take place. The decision as to which improvements can and will be made, and what actions will be implemented in order to close those gaps remains with the agency under assessment. The assessment process itself is not prescriptive. It does not dictate how an agency should be organized or how many levels of management it should have. It does not recommend what measures should be used or how leaders should act. It is a tool that provides the information that organizations need to make decisions.

The list of potential opportunities for improvement developed in the last stage may be very long, and it's likely that there will be more opportunities than can reasonably be addressed. The next task is to narrow them down to a smaller, more achievable set of opportunities that will form the basis for improvement plans.[1] The question is how to determine what improvements are most needed, desired, and achievable. Evaluating the opportunities and selecting the highest priorities may not be an easy process. People may view those opportunities for improvement that affect them or their ability to get their jobs done as the highest priority. Ruben (2005) describes it this way: "… the problems that matter to colleagues will be the ones they define as critical, and these may not be the same ones that preoccupy you or the administrators who created your program."[2] The goal, especially for an assessment process leader or facilitator, is to keep the attention focused on the organization as a whole, and what would provide the biggest benefit in helping the organization achieve its mission. As these priorities are negotiated, the result is a common agreement on an agenda for improvement.

While the final determination of priorities rests with the organization's leaders (Figure 6.1), the initial determination can be made by the assessment participants, who have the most information about how and why each potential opportunity was placed on the list. This initial prioritization can be done as part of an assessment workshop or as part of the activities of a project team or organization-wide team. Making clear exactly how prioritization will be done may be an important thing to communicate up front so as not to create false expectations.

Taking into consideration the relative strength of the organization in each category, the strategic plan or organizational goals, the available resources, and any other pertinent factors, the opportunities can be grouped into priority categories (high/medium/low) or ranked in order of priority. There are a number of different methods available for prioritization, some of which may be more suited than others to the assessment method in use (Figure 6.2).

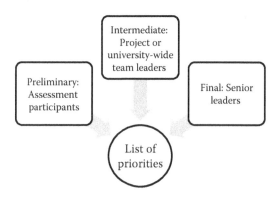

**Figure 6.1  Many parties can be part of the prioritization process, but the final determination of agency priorities belongs to the agency's leaders, who have to consider resource allocation, budgeting, constituents, and the priorities of those to whom they report.**

| | Workshop | Project Team | Organization-Wide Team |
|---|---|---|---|
| Consensus | | × | |
| Voting | × | × | × |
| Multivoting[3] | × | × | × |
| Survey of participants | | × | × |
| Survey of all employees | | × | × |

**Figure 6.2   Options for prioritization: Any of the options can be used with any of the assessment methods, but some are more suited to particular models.**

Surveys can be a particularly interesting way to determine organizational priorities. The use of electronic survey software allows process leaders to create a list of all possible options and ask respondents to rate the priority (very important, important, less important, not important). Distributing such a survey to all members of the organization brings those who were not able to participate in the first two stages of the assessment into the prioritization process in a way that can generate support for the process more than if they were made aware of the outcomes at the end of the process.

When making the final determination, it's also important to acknowledge that not all of the highest priorities may be able to be implemented. The scope of some of the improvement opportunities may mean that only a few can be implemented at one time due to resource limitations. Factors, such as workload, timing, and political considerations, also may play a role. Similarly, it is important to remember that not every improvement opportunity selected for implementation has to be the highest priority. While it is certainly important to determine the highest priority items for action, there also is value in selecting some low-hanging fruit; that is, some easily implemented and recognizable improvement opportunities. This demonstrates to the rest of the workforce that the process will result, as they were originally told, in some level of improvement. Small successes build support for the more difficult and, perhaps, more important and long-lasting changes that will result from the process as well.

## *Action Planning*

Once the task of establishing a list of priorities for implementation has been accomplished, the next step is to begin the project planning process for the selected projects. This first involves translating a statement of need into an actual project that will address the situation. Going back again to the constituent communication example, an opportunity for improvement that says: "There is no process for providing constituent feedback on projects to the project manager" can be phrased in terms of a project: "Design and implement a feedback process to ensure constituent feedback is provided to the project manager." Once the project has been defined, create a written action plan that specifies what is to be done, by when, and by whom. In developing action plans, it is important to define time frames for interim progress steps and project completion, processes and mechanisms for reporting progress, clear deliverables, and responsible parties.

This is the step where it is easiest for improvement processes to fall apart. Whether the assessment has taken a few days or several months or even a year or more, it's normal for people to go back to their regular work lives, at which point the improvement projects become of secondary importance compared to the everyday need to accomplish the regular mission of the organization. Therefore, it's important to designate who will track progress on the various plans, and that person may or may not be the same as the assessment project leader.

## Stage 4: Outcomes and Feedback

The final stage of the assessment process focuses on communicating the outcomes of the assessment process to those inside and outside the process. It's critical to inform the organization as a whole about both the progress and outcomes of the assessment, especially when all employees have not had access to the process.[4] This includes communicating to all employees the steps taken and the accomplishments achieved.

How will the outcomes be disseminated?
To whom will the information be provided?
What communication methods are most appropriate for different audiences?
How will feedback be incorporated in the assessment process?

The choice of a method for disseminating the information depends on the agency itself. Factors to be considered included the agency's size, the geographic distribution of employees, and available technology. The most important factor is not how you communicated the information, but the audience to whom you communicate it, in this case, to all employees. There are a number of reasons why is it important to disseminate the information that comes out of the assessment process:

■ The purpose of collecting the information used in the assessment is to provide the most comprehensive view of the current state of the organization so that it can be used for decision making. Sharing this information can have a positive impact on decision making outside the assessment process, by ensuring that people have access to more information than they might normally receive in the course of doing business.
■ It creates ownership of the process by the organization as a whole. Rather than being seen as the work product of a limited group or team of employees, sharing the outcomes makes everyone a part of the process.
■ It sets the stage for implementation by presenting the underlying logic for changes resulting from the assessment process.
■ It gives people an internal benchmark from which they can compare the impact of changes on future performance and effectiveness.
■ It demonstrates seriousness of purpose to employees. It indicates a willingness to change and demonstrates that their input was incorporated into the process and their concerns addressed to the greatest extent possible.
■ It provides a way to get information to those who, because of their role in the organization, might not otherwise have the opportunity to learn this information.
■ It provides an educational element by sharing information that will shape both staff and constituent perspectives on the way that the organization operates.
■ It opens the process to feedback, and can be used as a first step in establishing a feedback loop within the agency.

Disseminating information creates a basis for moving forward into implementation and periodic reassessment. Perhaps the most important aspect of providing this information is to educate staff about the process and its benefits, which in turn begins the process of creating a culture of assessment.

## BEST PRACTICE

**Use participants as ambassadors for what you are doing—**
Participants can be the best source of information about the potential of an assessment process to create positive change. Because communication is so important, encourage them to talk to others about the process, the information and how it is being obtained, and the results. This can dispel concerns and helps spread the information needed to bring about change.

## External Communication

Agency staff members are not necessarily the only audience for communicating the outcomes of an assessment. These results also can be presented to constituents. Constituents, on a regular basis, are making their own assessments of public sector performance, but those assessments may have little to do with actual performance, and more to do with how they perceive their access to government decision making. Proactive communication of assessment results can build trust in government's efforts to engage constituents in organizational improvement efforts. This also can apply to regulatory agencies or governing boards. In a 2008 audio conference sponsored by the International City/County Management Association (ICMA), Ellen Liston of

## BEST PRACTICE

**Share and educate—**Don't think of the information gained in an assessment as proprietary. Sharing information with other jurisdictions builds relationships that can be drawn upon in the future. Similarly, be certain to brief incoming leaders about how assessment has become part of the organizational culture.

You also can make use of process experts to communicate outcomes. The New Jersey Department of Environmental Protection, after a site visit by examiners for the New Jersey Quality Award, invited the lead examiner to come back and give a presentation to any interested agency employees to explain what they were looking for and what they found. Using a process expert to help explain the process and outcomes can add credibility and help people grasp the most important aspects of the assessment and its outcomes.

the Baldrige Award winning city of Coral Springs, Florida, talked about how they not only provide assessment information to their commission members, but do so in a workshop format where it can be reviewed and discussed.

## The Role of Change Management in Implementing Improvements

Implementing the desired improvements—regardless of the size and scope of those efforts—means introducing an element of change in the organization, a process that affects people, processes, and relationships. Incorporating an understanding of how change takes place can have a great deal of impact on the success of those implementation efforts.

Organizational change is the term used to describe the complex process through which current operations are modified to create a different and presumably more effective way of doing things, with the goal of reaching its best or optimal state of operation. While we may not stop to consider, in the midst of day-to-day operations, how change takes place, it can generally be said that the process of change is initiated when there is a difference between the current organization and its desired or planned condition, or, as Weisbord (1987) describes it, when there is "an incongruity between what they want or need and what they have."[5] The emphasis in both academic and popular management literature has not been on *whether* organizations need to change, but instead on *how* they change—understanding the reasons for change and the way in which it is designed, introduced, and implemented.

## The Process of Organizational Change

One of the most widely known models of organizational change is that developed by Kurt Lewin (Father of social psychology), a linear model that describes change efforts as a three-step process:

1. *Unfreezing* requires the organization to let go of its current way of doing business and consider what other possibilities there are for accomplishing their mission.
2. *Moving* means acting on the identified improvement plans, a time of transition when new ideas and processes are being introduced and integrated into the existing work operations of the organization. This can be the most difficult part of the process; in addition to determining what to change, and how to change it, leaders must understand the

importance of overcoming the inherent organizational forces pushing for the status quo.

3. *Refreezing* is when the organization restabilizes by incorporating the changes, including new processes, ideas, and ways of thinking, into the daily life of the organization.

Change can be incremental, taking place in small, planned steps, or transformational, substantially changing processes, structure, or the organization itself. No matter what the scope, change can be difficult because it requires employees to let go of what is familiar, adjust to a new situation, and then integrate the changes into their work. Anyone who has tried to initiate change in government knows that it is not always an easy thing to accomplish, despite the strength of the perceived need or the best of intentions. Government agencies are generally highly structured, regulated, and bureaucratic, which can make it difficult to gain consensus on new directions. The change process can be slow, which makes it difficult to meet public expectations for the speed of improvements. It also is highly dependent on the perspective and priorities of agency leaders.

## Challenges to Change Efforts

There are many potential barriers to change in public sector organizations. Identifying those barriers can help agencies anticipate the challenges and incorporate the information into planning for change initiatives. The inherent resistance of individuals to change is a commonly accepted belief in the field of organizational development and change management. Many people resent or even fear change because they are unsure about the impact on their immediate work processes, their jobs, and the organization as a whole. Uncertainty about what will happen, and the discomfort it causes, can be a powerful obstacle. As Mark Tucci of the New Jersey Department of Environmental Protection put it: "Middle managers don't like you to tamper with their world. They've learned how to manage the status quo."[6]

It is important as well to think about government agencies as systems, made up of many interdependent processes needed to provide services and programs and to maintain an internal infrastructure of support services. Because of this essential interdependence, changes made to any one part of the organization will affect, to a greater or lesser degree, all the other parts, as shown in Figure 6.3.

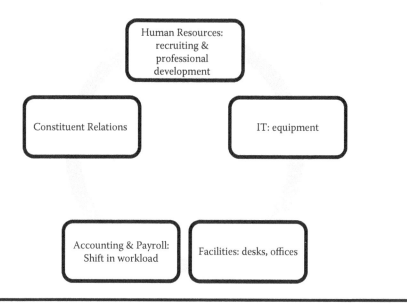

**Figure 6.3   Impact of change: Organizations as systems.**

The ability to implement changes desired by an organization also can be subject to externally generated priorities. Emergencies can call priorities into questions and drive the reallocation of resources by focusing public opinion on specific problems or incidents. The tragic 2007 bridge collapse in Minnesota created widespread public awareness of the state of the nation's infrastructure and brought demands from legislative leaders and constituents for immediate and extensive bridge inspections, despite the many state and local bridge inspection programs regularly conducted across the country, and generated calls for increased funding and priority shifting to enable investment in bridges and infrastructure.

## BEST PRACTICE

### Recognize the impact of change on the organization—
Allow things to stabilize after a change effort. Constant change can be difficult and often frustrating to leaders and staff alike. The idea that a government agency will always be changing is in sharp contrast to the beliefs of many managers and employees who think that if they can just get through implementing the current change initiative, things will get "back to normal." The difficult reality is that change is, in many ways, the normal condition of the agency.

## *Overcoming Resistance to Change*

A critical function of assessment is to support and enable such change, not only by providing the information that leads to identifying the improvements to be made, but also by using the process to build an understanding across the agency, among participants and nonparticipants, that change is needed. One of the most fundamental ways to approach and overcome resistance to change is by presenting people with sufficient credible information about the organization to enable them to see why the change is being enacted and why it is beneficial. The process of successful organizational change requires that people:

- believe that there are things that need to be changed, possibly because they have seen problems that continue to occur time after time
- believe that there is an advantage to changing, and that moving forward will be better than maintaining the status quo
- believe that change is possible within their organization

A frequent problem in change initiatives is an assumption by organizational leaders that staff members understand the reasons for change, yet this may not be true. These people may not have access to the same information as the decision makers and, therefore, may not perceive the underlying reasons for the change. They may not be aware of threats or opportunities that are driving the change effort. If people do not understand why change is taking place, they will be much less likely to accept it.

The success of change efforts also can be tied to how much the outcome differs from the way that an individual "sees" the organization. When people consider proposed changes, they will do so in the context of what they perceive to be the *identity* of the organization. An organization's identity, as described by Albert and Whetten (1985) is what the people who work in an organization see as its underlying purpose and central focus; what they believe makes it distinct from other similar organizations. People have a personal understanding of how they think the organization will behave in certain situations based on what they perceive to be its core values. Dutton and Dukerich (1991) suggest that this perception of organizational identity influences both the way that people interpret information that they receive and how they think about approaching and solving questions or issues. Organizational identity is created and reinforced every day through the nteraction that people have with co-workers, supervisors, and leaders, and through their experiences at work.

In practical terms, this means that one of the factors that should be considered in approaching improvement initiatives and change is whether the proposed outcomes will be in accordance or in conflict with what employees see as the identity of the organization. If they believe that the proposed changes are consistent with the agency's identity, they may be more willing to accept it. On the other hand, if they believe that a proposed change doesn't fit with the agency's identity, they may be less willing to support it and make the necessary adjustments—or they may actively oppose it.

Involving employees in the assessment process can help overcome resistance by providing an opportunity to both identify the issues and develop the changes to be implemented. The assessment process, through its emphasis on information collection and employee participation, enables leaders to build a knowledge base throughout the organization on which they can draw in order to act on the priorities for change. The process can facilitate change by reframing the way individuals and groups think about their work. It enables them to recognize different sets of priorities than they might otherwise consider.

## BEST PRACTICE

**Evaluate assessment efforts—** It's possible to add to the benefits of assessment and create an opportunity for increased organizational learning by incorporating a feedback loop. Adding follow-up interviews that assess the satisfaction of participants, nonparticipants, and organizational leaders with the assessment process itself provides an opportunity for double loop learning as people learn how to improve the process.

# Sustaining Organizational Assessment: Lessons Learned

Government, with its diverse responsibilities and far-reaching services, is part of the day-to-day lives of all Americans. The work performed by those who make their careers in government agencies plays a critical role in determining the quality of life for those who live, work, or engage in some way with their communities. Because of this, there are many compelling reasons why those who lead these agencies and those who work in public sector organizations must continue to improve their operations; not the least of which is that the challenges facing these organizations will continue to grow as the increasing demand for services struggles for balance against the available resources. Making the best possible use of these resources requires efficiency and effectiveness, and an appreciation for the need to examine not just outcomes, but organizations in order to see how they might be improved. The question facing government agencies is how to measure their processes, major work functions, and outcomes in an objective way that can:

- tell the story of government's successes and accomplishments
- be replicated so that results can be compared from year to year
- enable comparisons with public and private sector organizations
- measure the right things; that is, obtaining information and examining outcomes that represent the most important functions of the agency and which can lead to improvement
- identify the most critical needs for improvement
- measure progress in a way that is meaningful to constituents, legislators, and other groups

An organizational assessment gives you a picture of the agency at a moment in time that, while valuable, needs to be repeated in order to determine progress and identify next steps. Once you have successfully completed a cycle of assessment, planning, and improvement, the challenge is to sustain the effort. Efforts to link the outcomes of assessment processes to strategic planning and future budgets have not always been successful, but establishing links between those processes and making assessment part of the decision-making process may be the key to institutionalizing assessment efforts. Establish a perspective that looks at the organization as a whole; examines how its various parts, programs, and priorities interact; and use that information to create a culture in which people routinely look to see how they might make their agency more capable of serving the needs of its constituents. The challenge for government leaders, managers, and staff, then, is find a way to create a culture in which all employees think about whether there are better, more efficient, and more effective ways to serve the public. One of the long-term goals associated with the implementation of an assessment program is to make assessment a regular part of the way that the organization does business, and to create a management model based on the cycle of assessment, planning, and improvement.

The original work on which this workbook is based studied the process and the impact of implementing organizational assessment in three award-winning government agencies: one local, one state, and one federal. The City of Coral Springs, Florida, and the United States Army Armament Research, Development, and Engineering Center (ARDEC) were winners of the Baldrige National Quality Award in the first year of eligibility for government agencies. The New Jersey Department of Environmental Protection was a winner of the 2002 National Public Service Excellence Award. By studying their successes and the sustainability of their improvement efforts, we can learn important lessons to apply to future organizational assessment and improvement processes.

■ Take a **systematic approach** to assessment and improvement: All three agencies undertook assessments using a structured framework that identified the critical areas for evaluation and provided a process for collecting, analyzing, and acting on the information. After assessing the organization, each agency embarked on an effort to translate the knowledge gained into improvements. While results can be achieved from a single assessment, the road that each of these organizations followed prior to receiving an award generally took several years, during which the assessment and improvement cycle was repeated on an annual basis in order to build on the information received and the results achieved. Each year spent engaging in assessment and improvement increases staff knowledge about the process, about the level and type of information needed, and about how to use the information. The use of a structured process also facilitates comparisons from year to year and allows agencies to assess their progress over time.

■ Obtain **feedback from external sources:** All three agencies cited the external feedback that they received as a valuable source of information. Sources of feedback can include constituents, peer organizations, benchmarking consortia, and award programs. Coral Springs and ARDEC both incorporated information from their constituents as part of their assessment process, and all three engaged in some level of benchmarking. External feedback provided the agencies with a different perspective and a chance to see themselves as others—constituents, beneficiaries, and peers—see them. Feedback can be more formal, such as the feedback received from the award programs in response to applications and following site visits, or as informal as asking people who know the organization whether the information developed in an assessment "rings true."

■ **Engage employees** in the assessment process: A key theme in all three cases is the need to engage as many employees as possible in the process. Each of the organizations established a core team that was responsible for collecting and analyzing the information needed to assess the organization. In some cases, it was a dedicated assignment for a period of time, but most often it was done in conjunction with the team member's regular work assignments and responsibilities. Involvement extended beyond the core team, as other staff members functioned as writers, reviewers, site visit escorts, or as sources of information. Communication became a primary method of engagement for those who were not specifically involved in the process. Keeping employees involved in what was being done through presentations, training, and emails, and sharing the results with the entire organization, were some of the strategies used.

■ Understand that this is an **organizational commitment:** Assessment and improvement were not limited to certain processes or areas. There was a deliberate effort in all three agencies to make sure that all parts of their organization were involved. Creating a culture of assessment and improvement can require a shift in the existing organizational culture, which can include recognizing that government agencies have identifiable beneficiaries and constituents, accepting the need to share information across organizational lines, and stepping out of a day-to-day focus to understand that improvement is possible and desirable. Success for these agencies came from incorporating assessment and improvement into everyone's regular job processes by linking it to their jobs and making it part of their everyday work.

■ Recognize that this is a **learning process:** All of the organizations implemented some kind of training program for employees on quality practices and the assessment methodology. The skills required to assess an organization can be learned and improved on through subsequent assessments. They also supported staff members who wanted to go beyond a basic understanding of the processes by encouraging people to become trained as examiners and bring the information back to improve the assessment effort.

■ Have the **support of senior leaders:** The initial question in undertaking an assessment is whether your leadership team is committed to making a difference. The level of that support can make a real difference.

■ Finding ways to sustain a culture of assessment that **don't rely on a single champion:** Having a highly placed and visible champion in the organization can be extremely helpful to those implementing an assessment process. It provides a signal to those who hold the necessary resources (time, information, and people) that this effort is in the best interests of the agency. However, one of the challenges for assessment is finding ways to prevent programs from being linked to a particular person or political appointee and, therefore, subject to abandonment if that person leaves or the administration changes. Mark Tucci[6] of the New Jersey Department of Environmental Protection suggests that one strategy to do this is to communicate the benefits achieved through existing assessment programs to new administrators. Sustaining organizational assessment programs depends on the ability to prevent the disruption of these processes due to political changes. Those who would promote assessment in government need to be able to convey a sense of its importance to the internal operation and effectiveness of the organization and get both internal and external constituents to recognize that improvement is not political.

■ **Link Assessment to Strategic Planning efforts:** Government agencies at the federal, state, and local level routinely engage in planning and budgeting processes that rely on outcome data and performance measures to gauge their success in providing services. Assessment is often undertaken as prelude to preparing a strategic or business plan by providing the organization and the participants with knowledge about its current state. An assessment initiative also can be part of an actual strategic planning process by providing a model to be followed by the participants in defining the strengths, weaknesses, opportunities, and threats facing the organization.

■ Take steps to **institutionalize the process:** Even if the time frame is one or more years away, plant the idea that assessment is an ongoing process that will be conducted at regular intervals.

An organizational assessment can be tremendously beneficial to any government agency, but it is important to remember that it is a process, and requires planning and forethought. By carefully considering the operational and human resource factors, it is possible to successfully conduct an organizational assessment and meet the ongoing work requirements of the organization. In time, you can create a culture of assessment where efforts to constantly and carefully review the way in which you accomplish your organizational mission become part of day-to-day operations.

## Endnotes

1. The negotiation and consensus processes that took place in the information-gathering stage pay important dividends here. If the participants are in agreement on the challenges and opportunities facing the organization, it facilitates the selection of priorities for improvement and helps the organization to focus improvement efforts where they are most beneficial.
2. Ruben (2005), p. 384.
3. Multivoting refers to the process in which there are multiple rounds of voting, with the elimination each round of the least popular option.
4. While smaller organizations or units may involve their entire staff, many organizations find it difficult, if not impossible, to include every employee in the assessment process because of the sheer size of the staff or the available time frame. In this case, it is particularly important to share the outcomes.
5. Weisbord (1987), p. 229.
6. Interview with Mark Tucci, March 17, 2008.

# Glossary

**Appreciative Inquiry:** A method of evaluation and assessment that, rather than looking at poor performance, focuses attention on times and events when the organization has performed well, and looks at what made those successes possible.

**Assessment:** A systematic process for examining an organization to create a shared understanding of the current state of those elements that are critical to the successful achievement of its purposes.

**Baldrige National Quality Award ("Baldrige"):** A widely recognized program, operated by the National Institute of Standards and Technology of the United States Department of Commerce, which is designed to recognize excellence in organizations by assessing their performance in seven categories that represent critical organizational functions. (See also Malcolm Baldrige National Quality Award.)

**Benchmarking:** The process of comparing one organization, or the functions, processes and results of that organization to another; commonly used to identify, study, and emulate best practices or to compare an organization to its peers or the leading agencies in its field.

**Beneficiaries:** Those people and organizations who benefit from the impact of the work of government, either as direct users of government services or through the general benefit to society of government's actions.

**Communication:** The exchange of information in order to create shared meaning.

**Consensus:** A process through which individual participants reach an agreement that can be supported by all parties involved.

**Constituents:** Those people and organizations that have an interest in the operation of government.

**Continuous Improvement:** A way of conducting operations so that processes are continually reviewed for opportunities to improve the functioning of the organization.

**Core Process:** A series of systematic steps that carry out the activities of a core program.

**Core Program:** A program that carries out the mission of the organization.

**Criteria for Performance Excellence:** A set of questions in seven major categories used in the Baldrige National Quality Program to collect the information needed for an organizational assessment process.

**Dashboard:** A visual display of performance measures that allows the user to quickly determine the current state of a selected set of critical indicators.

**Deployment:** The process through which a particular practice is adopted throughout an organization; it may also refer to the extent to which a practice is deployed.

**Diffusion of Innovation:** The process through which information about new ideas is communicated, adopted, and accepted by the members of a group.

**Excellence in Higher Education:** A program for organizational assessment in colleges and universities that is an adaptation of the Baldrige National Quality Program to include the culture and language of higher education.

**Facilitator:** A person who supports the assessment process by providing direction to groups as they engage in assessment activities.

**Government Performance and Results Act (GPRA):** A federal government program enacted to improve the performance of federal agencies.

**Improvement Plan:** A plan of action created as an outcome of an assessment process, which identifies the highest priority opportunities for improvement and assigns specific responsibilities, time frames, and action steps to enact the proposed improvements.

**Improvement Priorities:** Those opportunities for improvement resulting from an assessment that have been selected as the highest priorities for implementation.

**Incremental Change:** A change process in which adjustments are made to existing processes and in which the intended outcome is visible to the members of the organization.

**Interpersonal Communication:** The process and methods through which individuals communicate with each other individually or in groups.

**Leaders:** The person or persons who are identified as leaders for purposes of assessing the performance of organizational leadership.

**Malcolm Baldrige National Quality Award:** An award presented annually to recognize excellence in business, nonprofit, healthcare, and education organizations. (See also Baldrige National Quality Program.)

**Mission:** The defining purpose for which an organization exists.

**Mission Statement:** A statement of purpose that is generally written and disseminated to employees and constituents.

**Negotiation:** The process through which two or more parties discuss their differences in order to reach common agreement on an issue.

**Operationalize:** A way of presenting a concept or idea so that it can be understood and measured.

**Opportunities for Improvement:** Those organizational structures, processes, practices, or procedures that have been identified in an assessment process as having the potential to benefit from change and improvement.

**Organizational Assessment:** A systematic process for examining an organization in order to create a shared understanding of the current state of the factors that are critical to the successful achievement of its purposes.

**Organizational Change:** The process through which an organization moves from its current state to a different and more desirable state.

**Organizational Climate:** The current state of the organization as perceived by its employees, encompassing morale, perceived treatment, and interpersonal relationships.

**Organizational Communication:** The process through which members of the organization share information in order to create meaning.

**Organizational Culture:** The shared values, beliefs, and norms held by an organization.

**Organizational Development:** A process that uses behavioral science to create organizational and personal learning and build a case for change in organizations.

**Organizational Identification:** The way in which an individual views his or her connection to the organization.

**Organizational Identity:** What the members of the organization believe to be the definition of its purposes and central characteristics.

**Outcome Measures:** A set of metrics that describe the outcomes achieved by the organization.

**Participant:** An individual who takes part in and/or plays an active role in an organizational assessment process.

**Performance Assessment Rating Tool (PART):** A federal government program for evaluating agency performance and goal achievement.

**Performance Measurement:** A systematic process for identifying key performance indicators and measuring the relative progress over a period of time.

**Performance Measures:** The key performance indicators selected to represent progress toward organizational goals and objectives.

**Process:** A series of steps through which an organization carries out a specific program or action.

**Process Improvement:** A quality methodology in which processes are systematically examined to determine opportunities for improvement.

**Program:** A set of operations used to enact a set of goals and objectives.

**Quality:** A state in which the operations, processes, and programs of an organization are enacted in a way that produces the optimum levels of achievement.

**Quality Improvement:** A philosophy in which organizations and their programs and processes are reviewed, analyzed, and revised in order to improve the outcomes.

**Robust:** A description used to indicate that a program or process is particularly strong, successful, or thoroughly deployed throughout an organization.

**Self-Assessment:** An assessment process that uses the members of an organization as the participants and source of information as opposed to external assessors, such as a consultant or auditor.

**Strategic Planning:** A systematic process through which the members and leaders of an organization determine the goals, objectives, strategies, and action plans necessary to move the organization to its desired level of performance.

**Strengths:** Programs, processes, or behaviors that are performed well.

**Support Process:** A series of steps that enacts a support program.

**Support Program:** A program that provides support services, such as human resources, accounting, facilities management, or information technology, in support of the core programs of the organization.

**SWOT Analysis:** An assessment tool in which the participants compile lists of the strengths, weaknesses, opportunities, and threats that they see in the organization.

**Systems Approach or Systems Theory:** Recognizing that organizations are made up of various interlocking systems and examining the way that they function together.

**Total Quality Management (TQM):** A way of conducting and managing operations that emphasizes the review and improvement of performance and processes so that the best possible quality can be obtained.

**Transformational Change:** An organizational change process in which major changes are instituted, which are discontinuous with current operations.

**Values:** Those personal and organizational characteristics that are expected of the members of an organization; those characteristics, attitudes, and approaches that the members of the organization have the right to expect from each other in the performance of their jobs.

**Vision:** A statement of what the organization sees as its ultimate goal or performance.

# Appendix A

## Understanding the Public Sector Assessment and Improvement (PSAI) Model

The Public Sector Assessment and Improvement (PSAI) Model (Figure A.1) is made up of seven assessment categories. This narrative is a supplement to the worksheets provided in the workbook, and provides a more in-depth look at the reasoning behind the categories.

## The Human Factor Group: Interpersonal and Communication Competence

### Category 1: Leadership

Leadership is the art of accomplishing more than the science of management says is possible.

**Colin Powell (Powell and Persico, 1996)**

Leaders in government organizations face an interesting set of challenges. At best, they have the potential to shape entire societies through their actions. At worst, they are charged with leading organizations whose missions may be determined by people outside their organization, to provide services people don't always want, to people who have no choice but to use them. In government, leaders may be elected or appointed to their positions, or they may be career employees who have risen to leadership positions. Although we tend to think of the formal leaders, there can be leaders at many levels throughout the organization: senior administrators, directors, managers, bureau chiefs, committee or task force chairpersons, team leaders, and project coordinators.

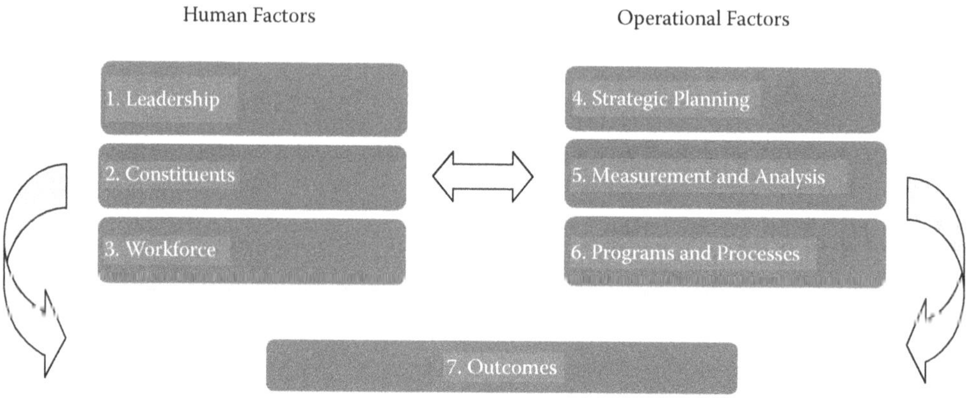

Human Factors                Operational Factors

**Figure A.1   The Public Sector Assessment and Improvement (PSAI) model.**

One of the best descriptions of the trust that society places in the leaders of government organizations, and the responsibility that goes with it is the Athenian Oath, which historians tell us was taken by the young men of the City of Athens when they reached the age of 17. While there are some variations in translation, one passage appears consistently: the commitment that "we will transmit this City, not only not less, but greater and more beautiful than it was transmitted to us."[3]

## The Athenian Oath

*We will never bring disgrace on this our City by an act of dishonesty or cowardice.*

*We will fight for the ideas and Sacred things of the City both alone and with many.*

*We will revere and obey the City's laws, and will do our best to incite a like reverence and respect in those above us who are prone to annul them or set them at naught.*

*We will strive increasingly to quicken the public's sense of civic duty.*

*Thus in all ways we will transmit this City, not only not less, but greater and more beautiful than it was transmitted to us.*

*We will strive increasingly to quicken the public's sense of civic duty.*

There are certain aspects of leadership that are commonly used to represent some of the key elements for success in individual and organizational leadership in the public sector. These include:

- Focusing the attention and energy of the workforce on the organization's mission, vision, values, plans, and goals.
- Educating staff about the opportunities and challenges facing public sector organizations, and supporting the need for both performance measurement and continuous improvement.
- Motivating staff and promoting teamwork and collaborative problem solving.
- Creating a sense of urgency about the need to take those actions critical to securing the welfare of the public.
- Demonstrating a respect for constituents and beneficiaries, and supporting the role that these groups play in the formation of public policy.

Key to the success of organizational leaders is the need to synchronize what they say with what they do. By exemplifying organizational values and principles in their actions, they model the behavior they wish to inspire in the remainder of the organization. Responsible conduct is particularly important in government. Leaders in the public sector must demonstrate the highest levels of ethical and socially responsible behavior. Acting ethically in one's personal behavior is only one aspect of this requirement. Leaders must be alert for ethical challenges—particularly conflicts of interest—that face the organization as a whole, and take steps to establish a clear expectation of ethical behavior among everyone in the workforce. Leaders must demonstrate socially responsible behavior, which considers the impacts caused by the operation of the organization. These things (ranging from, for example, pollution risks from salt storage or waste facility locations to safe driving by employees) that either allow you or prevent you from being a "good neighbor" and a responsible presence in the community in which you are located.

This category covers the actions of leaders in directing the day-to-day and long-term operations of the agency, maintaining a clear focus on the mission, supporting the workforce in accomplishing its goals, and establishing ways to incorporate and address the needs and expectations of the constituents and beneficiaries that they serve. This category considers leadership structure, practices, and ethics.

## *Category 2: Constituents*

This category looks at how the agency identifies the needs, expectations, perspectives, and satisfaction level of the agency's constituents: the individuals, groups, publics, and organizations for which you provide programs or services. It considers the way the agency identifies and builds relationships with constituents and how it determines their needs, expectations, and satisfaction levels. The term constituents can include:

■ Those who benefit—either individually, as part of a larger constituency, or as members of society as a whole—from the agency's programs and services.
■ A small organization that is part of the agency under consideration, e.g., a division or unit.
■ A different government office or program that is dependent on the programs, services, regulation, or funding provided by another government agency.
■ Those who provide support and funding for programs or services, including taxpayers, legislators, other levels of government, or organizations who provide grants.
■ Those who provide materials, contracted services, or expertise that is essential to accomplishing the work.

For technical or program units, the list of constituents may include the public at large; schools; businesses; travelers through or visitors to the jurisdiction; state and federal funding agencies; advisory boards; local, state, and federal government; regulatory agencies; the citizens or other residents of a community or state; the media; and other groups. For example, if the organization under consideration is an entire agency—such as a department of state government, a whole municipality, or a federal agency—the list of constituents would include the residents of the state or community; members of the business community; educational institutions; advisory or governing boards; other local, state, and federal governments; regulatory agencies; the media; external groups that enable the agency to accomplish its work, such as suppliers, consultants, and contractors; and others. If the organization being considered is a public works division with a mission involving construction and maintenance of municipal infrastructure, the list would likely include community residents, state government, procurement offices o funding agencies, members of engineering or public works firms, and other municipal departments it works with on a daily or on a project-specific basis.

The concept of constituent focus is equally important for administrative departments that provide programs and services within the agency, such as human resources, budget and accounting, information technology, equipment or fleet maintenance, or other similar services. For these units, the constituents would typically be the technical or program departments for which they provide services. For a facilities department, for example, the list of constituents would include departments or offices for which custodial, maintenance, or construction services are provided, as well as vendors and suppliers who are needed in order to provide these services.

In government organizations, the need to address the perspective of constituents or beneficiaries is often overlooked. Those who work in government often have a difficult time thinking of people and groups who benefit from their services as "customers" because it implies that they are "shopping" or making a choice to engage in business with that agency. Many government agencies provide services to groups that have no choice as to whether they wish to take advantage of the services. For example, individuals cannot decide to "opt out" of the tax collection activities of the federal, state, or municipal government. External groups and individuals also may have no choice when it comes to who provides a service—an individual who wants to receive a check for unemployment benefits cannot go to another "vendor" other than a public agency to receive the service. Nor are services restricted to a particular group of "customers." In government, perhaps more than in any other sector, the societal nature of the work means that people are likely to be beneficiaries of an agency's services even if they are not direct "customers" or consumers of those services.

Input from constituents is essential to determine whether the goals of efficiency and effectiveness in programs and services are being realized. To be successful in developing and maintaining good working relationships with constituents, effort must be directed to learning about the perspectives, needs, and expectations of these individuals, groups, and organizations. Information from constituents and beneficiaries can be used to evaluate current programs and services, to identify needed improvements in communication about existing programs and services, or to create new programs and services.

This information also is needed to identify and address constituent dissatisfaction, which can result from differences between the expected and the actual level of service, gaps in service or in populations served, or lack of access (physical or electronic) to services. Many constituent groups make assessments of the work being performed by public sector organizations, and all of these judgments have an important impact on the agency's credibility, which in turn affects the ability to accomplish the mission. The manner in which a government agency responds to individuals who need financial assistance, housing, or road reconstruction following a natural disaster, such as a hurricane, can translate into trust that engenders the support of the community during normal work operations. Once lost, such credibility and respect are difficult to regain. Failure to listen to constituents can translate into dissatisfied citizens who can lobby against and delay projects, invoke media support, and engage in legal challenges that tie the hands of a government agency. Moreover, external judgments about the quality of a state, local, or federal government agency or program can translate into financial support, in terms of the allocation of often limited funding streams, that is critical to the work and the well-being of the agency.

One of the critical success factors in achieving a high level of organizational performance is to have a clear understanding of the needs and wants of those served. This includes those who benefit directly from products and services and those who benefit indirectly. It applies to others who also have an interest in these services. Many of the existing tools for assessing organizations, including the Baldrige program, specifically include customer feedback as part of the assessment process. Government is becoming increasingly more sophisticated in identifying constituents and beneficiaries and figuring out how to incorporate them into the process.

## Category 3: Workforce

This category focuses on the agency's most valuable resource: its people. It considers how the agency manages, supports, and develops the workforce so that it can use its full potential to support the mission, vision, and plans. Excellence in the public sector depends on the ability of staff members to deliver services in a competent, effective, and efficient way. It relies on staff knowledge and expertise, combined with the ability and desire to work collectively for the public good. Therefore, it is important to create an organizational culture that encourages high-quality practices, and which both enables and motivates people to achieve high performance levels. The organization has to build and maintain a climate that values excellence, diversity, collaboration, learning, and personal and professional development. Just as important, workplaces must provide environmentally safe work ocations and practices as well as workplaces that safeguard the security of he workforce.

There is often a disconnect between the public perception of the government workforce and the reality of the excellent level of public service provided. From the perspective of government employees, they believe the public does not understand the challenges of public service or the complexity of their jobs.

Creating an effective public sector workplace requires supportive leadership, effective management practices, attention to workforce planning, and he organizational culture, recognition, and appropriate professional developmental opportunities. The work systems and practices implemented by he organization must promote effectiveness and efficiency while taking nto account the needs of the workforce. Government faces some unique challenges compared to the other sectors. Recruitment can be inherently more difficult for those government organizations where civil service regulations, that are designed to create a level playing field instead result in very generic job categories that hamper recruitment by making it difficult to obtain needed skill sets, or when complex recruitment procedures take so ong to implement that qualified candidates are lost to jobs in other sectors. Restructuring jobs or revising job descriptions to match a rapidly changing external environment is often a slow process that results in a mismatch between the skills needed and the skills recruited. Compensation is subject to public scrutiny, and the types of financial incentives or rewards that might be available in business, such as bonuses, incentive pay, or pay for performance, are not often available.

A systematic method for identifying staff expectations, perspectives, priorities, and satisfaction or dissatisfaction, is needed, along with a process for responding to concerns as they are identified. In this atmosphere, employee development becomes one of the primary tools to accomplish the work of the agency. The focus on employee development must include all staff groups, including the frontline employees who play a crucial role. Their behavior enables the organization to deliver services and accomplish its goals, while their interactions with constituents form the basis of public impressions. These impressions have a major impact on the perceived credibility of the organization and the satisfaction of groups served, which in turn, impacts the availability of human and financial resources. Government organizations can be hampered by a reluctance to invest in workforce development. They often hesitate to spend public funds on staff development, the concern being a perception by leaders and by constituents that such expenditures take funding away from the programs that constitute their "real business."

The need for strong leaders at all levels of government organizations, in both technical and administrative areas, is clear if government is to address the challenges it faces. However, many government agencies have been slow to adopt workforce initiatives, such as succession planning, workforce planning, and structured leadership development. Professional development, including leadership development, has long been neglected in the public sector, and expenditures for training generally fall far behind those of the private sector. Instead, the tendency is to promote those who have excelled in technical areas higher and higher up the chain of command. This approach can be shortsighted; although there are exceptions, the best technicians do not always make the best leaders. When dealing with an extremely stable workforce, and human resource practices shaped by the requirements of civil service systems, combined with limited incentives and disincentives related to performance, a lack of commitment to professional development can be a real problem. The skills and knowledge required to lead people, set forth a vision and goals, manage effectively, and inspire people to achieve the goals and priorities of the organization may already exist to some degree, but they can always be improved through education. A more desirable approach is to define the desired competencies for managers and leaders, and then to provide the kind of development opportunities that will identify and develop individuals to become effective leaders.

## The Operational Factors: Enabling the Work of the Organization

The second set of categories in the PSAI model is the Operational factors. These categories—strategic planning, measurement and information, and programs and processes—describe the way in which the work of the organization is accomplished.

### Category 4: Strategic Planning

Strategic planning is one of the foremost tools available to government organizations in creating and maintaining alignment between human and financial resources and the goals to be achieved at each level. It provides a way or agencies to translate the mission, as explained in its legislative mandate or enabling regulations, into direction and priorities. A strategic plan can serve as a compass that guides staff members in decision making. It provides a way for leaders to communicate the mission throughout the organization.

As important as strategic planning is, it can be overlooked in the press of day-to-day work operations. Many people believe that strategic planning is a time-consuming process, which results in a document that will "sit on a shelf" or that it is necessary only to meet budget requirements. Instead, a well-constructed strategic plan will identify the most critical opportunities facing the organization. It validates the investment of resources into those programs and services. At the same time, strategic planning enables leaders to identify those functions that are no longer linked to accomplishing the core mission, and sets the stage for shifting resources away from functions the agency may be used to performing, but which no longer add value.

Creating an actionable plan is the measure of an effective strategic planning process. Although it can require an investment of time, strategic planning can return that time many times over by focusing attention on the most important functions of the agency. The challenge for government leaders is to construct a strategic plan that:

- identifies the "critical few," the most important goals of the organization
- identifies strategies to transform the agency to meet upcoming priorities and future challenges
- aligns functions and resources (financial, human, technological) with goals
- appropriately allocates resources among competing priorities
- translates priorities into action plans
- contains processes to measure progress and make adjustments as needed

This category looks at the manner in which the mission is translated into a set of goals, and how the agency develops and implements short- and long-term plans and strategies to advance those goals. It also reviews how these plans and goals are disseminated throughout the organization, and how progress on plans and goals is assessed. In addition to goals and plans, this category also looks at the values of the organization, which might be defined as the attributes that employees can expect from their co-workers as they perform their jobs.

## *Category 5: Measurement and Analysis*

The availability and effective use of information is critical to all components of organizational excellence. A fundamental use of data and information is to measure or assess organizational performance. Such information may be used to evaluate the quality of programs and services and the organization's relationships with the groups it serves, as well as such internal factors as the workplace climate, level of staff satisfaction, and operational effectiveness. One of the major benefits of developing integrated measures of performance is that it helps the organization define excellence, and creates a common understanding among the leadership, employees, and constituents of how performance will be assessed.

Agencies develop performance indicators, or measures, to translate the mission, vision, values, plans, and goals into metrics that can be used to evaluate how well they are doing. Measures can be developed for every category in the PSAI model. In this category, organizations are asked to examine how they decide—from all the possible measures available—which performance measures are important. They also are asked how they identify the information needed, whether it is available, and how to collect the necessary data.

Performance measures are used to monitor progress on plans and goals, and to compare current results to the accomplishments from previous years. They can be used as well to draw comparisons between outcomes in one organization and those in another. By comparing measurement and performance data, agencies can learn from other public sector organizations and, where appropriate, from organizations in other sectors as well. This process of comparing processes and outcomes against those of other organizations is called benchmarking. Comparisons may be with similar government organizations in other geographic locations and/or with other types of organizations that have comparable processes or activities to those of your unit. For example, for a state government agency, facilities or purchasing processes may be compared to similar processes at peer organizations in another state or with organizations in other sectors. Comparisons with recognized leaders in government and/or with leaders in business, healthcare, or higher education can provide a basis for setting goals for the organization.

This category also examines how the agency shares and utilizes information, knowledge, and expertise internally and externally. The question becomes what—and how much—information to share to convey a sense of the current status without overwhelming people with data that is so extensive as to be meaningless. Many organizations identify a small set of core measures that are vital to accomplishing the mission of the organization or key to identifying and communicating the success of a particular program.

Ideally, the performance measures selected should:

■ reflect the mission, goals, plans, and priorities of the agency, department, or program
■ measure factors that influence the decision making of constituents, including those for whom services or programs are provided and those who determine the scope and funding of the agency's activities
■ provide a sense of accountability
■ be widely accessible and easy to understand
■ meet external reporting requirements
■ involve members of the organization in determining what to measure and why

Performance measures for programs, services, and activities should indicate progress toward achievement of performance goals or meeting target levels of service provided as well as quality, effectiveness, and efficiency. Performance indicators that measure the quality of relationships with constituents should include factors that are important to the groups and organizations served. These indicators might be based on results of surveys or focus groups with constituents or legislators. Also potentially useful are indirect measures, such as complaints or suggestion received, or positive or negative media attention. Indicators of human resource/staff satisfaction and workplace climate might include the results of surveys or interviews, retention, turnover rates, absenteeism, or analysis of exit interviews.

## Category 6: Programs and Processes

Every government organization carries out its mission through its programs and services. This category looks at the programs administered by the agency to provide the services required to serve its constituents and the processes through which those programs are carried out. The missions assigned to government agencies have grown, sometimes incrementally, through the addition of programs, services, or constituents, and sometimes through significant transformation, such as combining departments or consolidating jurisdictions to address resources issues or increase efficiency. Such changes require that agencies rethink the mission and identify what changes in priorities, structure, programs, and processes must be made within the agency to carry out the mission. They also must consider whether the core programs are valid, and whether the processes through which they are enacted are still effective.

Every organization has a set of programs that are essential to accomplishing the mission. These programs are referred to as *core programs*. Programs are carried out through processes, which can be defined as a sequence of action steps that constitute a work activity. The processes that are directly responsible for carrying out the core programs of the organization are called *core processes*. Core processes are those for which the organization has particular expertise. For technical units, core work processes typically include activities directly associated with the specific discipline of the agency, such as planning, engineering, social work, healthcare, or workforce development.

Organizations also have administrative functions that support the accomplishment of core programs, and that are necessary to the effective and efficient operation of the organization. The processes through which these functions are carried out are called *support processes*. Often, these processes are invisible to external groups. Examples of operational support processes would include recruiting and hiring, conducting performance reviews, training, purchasing equipment and supplies, coordinating repairs and maintenance, facility scheduling, preparing work materials, and scheduling and conducting meetings. Financial support processes might include fiscal management, budget development, grants development, and grants management.

Leaders and managers must ensure that the staff members who are charged with implementing the core and support programs and processes maintain a focus on the organization's goals and the needs of constituents. It is very common for individual staff members to be knowledgeable only about their own job and feel detached from the overall purposes of their department or the agency. When this happens, the individual tends to focus only on the part of the process that he or she performs, instead of looking at the whole process from start to finish. More often than not, core and major processes involve the work of individuals in more than one department or program. The interdepartmental—or, as it is often termed, *cross functional*—nature of work is apparent even in many basic activities.

Take, for example, the sequence of events in recruiting, hiring, and orienting new staff. The recruitment–hiring–orientation process, at a minimum, involves the department that has a vacancy to fill and the Human Resources Department. It also could involve the Equal Employment Opportunity Office and the Finance/Budget Department, as well as leaders who might have to approve the hiring. Add to that the support areas that need to identify office space and order and install computers.

Processes can be documented and analyzed to identify the specific steps involved, the sequence in which they are performed, and the people or departments responsible for each activity to determine how it might be improved. A focus on processes and outcomes, instead of on individual job duties, helps to overcome the tendency to look at the organization in "silos."

In some cases, organizational programs and processes require collaboration with external groups and organizations. Depending on the mission of the agency, examples might include collaborative relationships with other government organizations, universities, or communities. Examples of collaborative programs might include health initiatives between a state health department and a community hospital, or a recruiting partnership between a government agency and a local high school, community college, or university.

The emphasis in this category is on how these programs are designed, and how their corresponding processes are standardized, documented, monitored, and continually improved to achieve the highest possible levels of effectiveness and efficiency and to meet the needs and expectations of the groups being served.

## Category 7: Results

The goal for any government agency is to fulfill its core mission and serve its constituents effectively and efficiently. In government, where the decision to add, eliminate, or expand programs is not based on profit or loss statements, organizations must still measure their accomplishments against the mission, vision, plans, and goals to determine whether a level of organizational excellence is being achieved. Category 5 (Measurement and Analysis) focused on identifying the key measures, or indicators, of organizational performance and effectiveness. It asks what should be measured. In Category 7, the actual information collected for each of those measures or indicators is examined. These data, referred to here as *outcomes*, is compared to outcomes for other time periods or from other agencies to determine the level of organizational performance. Both current outcomes and outcomes over time can be examined.

This category does not consider how the work is done or how the mission and goals are carried out. Instead, the results category asks *what* the results were: *How well* was the work accomplished? Essentially, it asks what was found when the measures were taken. It includes results that document outcomes and achievements in each of the first six categories: leadership, constituents, workforce, strategic planning, measurement and analysis, and programs and processes. Documentation on results in each of these areas is needed for organizational self-assessment, planning, goal setting, and process improvement. It is also extremely valuable for communicating the accomplishments of the organization to internal and external constituencies. Presenting results and outcomes is a good way to "tell the story" of an agency and its accomplishments, which, in turn can generate support and additional resources.

This information can be used to improve the organization by:

- comparing results against goals established in the planning process to assess progress and plan improvements
- comparing results against previous years to determine trends
- comparing results against other government organizations.

# Appendix B

## The Public Sector Assessment and Improvement Model
## Short Form/Pilot Assessment

Based on the same Public Sector Assessment and Improvement (PSAI) model, the short form provides a way for agencies to:

- use a pilot project to build support for a full assessment
- conduct a preliminary assessment to determine organizational readiness
- undertake a quick assessment to determine priority areas on which to focus a full assessment

This abbreviated version of the PSAI model is in questionnaire format. It consists of statements about values, information, or behaviors that would, generally speaking, predict positive outcomes in a full assessment. Participants are asked to estimate whether each statement:

- is a valid description of the organization being assessed
- is a valid description of many parts of the organization
- is a valid description of some parts of the organization
- is not a valid description of the organization

# PSAI Pilot Survey

Human Factors

## 1. Leadership

| | Valid in all parts | Valid in many parts | Valid in some parts | Not valid |
|---|---|---|---|---|
| Leaders are visible to and accessible to members of the organization | O | O | O | O |
| Leaders have made their priorities clear throughout the organization | O | O | O | O |
| Leaders exhibit a focus on beneficiaries and constituents | O | O | O | O |
| Leaders have a commitment to ethical behavior | O | O | O | O |

## 2. Constituents

| | Valid in all parts | Valid in many parts | Valid in some parts | Not valid |
|---|---|---|---|---|
| The major constituent groups can be readily identified | O | O | O | O |
| Information about the most critical needs and expectations of constituents is collected and shared | O | O | O | O |
| Constituent information is incorporated into planning efforts | O | O | O | O |
| Constituent satisfaction with services is assessed on a regular basis | O | O | O | O |
| Performance measures include expectations for constituent service | O | O | O | O |
| Attention is paid to whether constituents have access to services | O | O | O | O |

# PSAI Pilot Survey

## 3. Workforce

| | Valid in all parts | Valid in many parts | Valid in some parts | Not valid |
|---|---|---|---|---|
| A process exists to identify current and future workforce needs | ○ | ○ | ○ | ○ |
| Core competencies have been identified for all employee groups or job titles | ○ | ○ | ○ | ○ |
| Recruitment processes support diversity | ○ | ○ | ○ | ○ |
| Excellence in individual and team performance is supported and recognized | ○ | ○ | ○ | ○ |
| Professional development opportunties are available to all employee groups | ○ | ○ | ○ | ○ |
| Workplace safety and security are assessed on a regular basis | ○ | ○ | ○ | ○ |
| Practices are in place to insure the workplace is free from discrimination and harassment | ○ | ○ | ○ | ○ |

# PSAI Pilot Survey

## 4. Strategic Planning

| | Valid in all parts | Valid in many parts | Valid in some parts | Not valid |
|---|---|---|---|---|
| The organization has a formal mission statement which is available to leaders, staff, and constituents | ○ | ○ | ○ | ○ |
| The vision that leaders have for the organization has been shared with and is known to staff | ○ | ○ | ○ | ○ |
| The organization's core values have been defined and communicated to staff | ○ | ○ | ○ | ○ |
| There is a formal, documented strategic planning process | ○ | ○ | ○ | ○ |
| Staff input and feedback are included in the planning process | ○ | ○ | ○ | ○ |
| The planning process aligns human and fiscal resources with identified goals | ○ | ○ | ○ | ○ |
| The strategic plan is communicated throughout the organization | ○ | ○ | ○ | ○ |

## 5. Measurement and Analysis

| | Valid in all parts | Valid in many parts | Valid in some parts | Not valid |
|---|---|---|---|---|
| Information about major work programs and processes is collected and disseminated for use | ○ | ○ | ○ | ○ |
| Safeguards are in place to protect data security and employee/constituent privacy | ○ | ○ | ○ | ○ |
| Performance measures are used to determine progress against the mission, plans, and goals | ○ | ○ | ○ | ○ |
| Data and information are used to compare current outcomes with the outcomes from previous years | ○ | ○ | ○ | ○ |
| Information is compared (benchmarked) against that of other organizations | ○ | ○ | ○ | ○ |

# PSAI Pilot Survey

## 6. Programs and Processes

|  | Valid in all parts | Valid in many parts | Valid in some parts | Not valid |
|---|---|---|---|---|
| The major processes associated with core programs and services are documented and reviewed on a regular basis | O | O | O | O |
| Performance measures are used to assess the efficiency and effectiveness of core processes | O | O | O | O |
| Processes and programs make the best possible use of technology | O | O | O | O |

## 7. Outcomes

**For each of the PSAI categories, how do the available performance outcomes compare to the information for the previous year?**

|  | Much more positive | Somewhat more positive | Same/level | Somewhat more negative | Much more negative |
|---|---|---|---|---|---|
| Leadership | O | O | O | O | O |
| Constituents | O | O | O | O | O |
| Workforce | O | O | O | O | O |
| Strategic Planning | O | O | O | O | O |
| Measurement and Analysis | O | O | O | O | O |
| Programs and Processes | O | O | O | O | O |

# Appendix C

## Exercises/Sample Training Program

These exercises can be used to stimulate discussion in organizations considering an assessment, or as part of a training program.

1. You are the director of Child Services in a large human services agency, and you believe that an assessment process would be helpful in improving the way that the agency as a whole operates. You raise the issue with the newly appointed head of the agency. He doesn't reject the idea, but it clearly isn't high on his list of priorities. You feel strongly that it would help your area, in particular, as well as the rest of the agency. What actions could you take?
2. The leaders of your agency have decided to implement an organizational assessment and you are directed to prepare a communication plan that details how information concerning the proposed assessment will be made available to employees. What types of communication will you use, and to whom will they be directed? Draft an announcement from your agency head explaining what will happen and why.
3. You are the team leader for an assessment process. Consider and explain the steps you would take to identify the best internal and external information sources.
4. You have been assigned to develop information about performance measures available in the public sector. Think about three government agencies at different levels in the same field: the U.S. Department of Education, a state Department of Education, and a local school board. What performance measures would be most important to each? Would they have any performance measures in common?

5. Using the Public Sector Assessment and Improvement (PSAI) model, write a proposal for applying it to your organization, including anticipated resources, time frames, and methodology.

6. You are charged with implementing an assessment process in a transportation agency that includes many different occupational groups. There are four primary groups that you wish to include in the assessment process: engineers, community relations specialists, human resource specialists, and highway maintenance staff. How would you structure the process in a way that recognizes the constituents of each group, differing priorities, and different levels of availability? What factors must be taken into consideration?

7. One type of information that exists in an agency is the stories that are shared between employees and which help shape the culture and identity of the agency. What are some of the stories told in and about your organization of which you are personally aware? What are some of the stories told in your area to "set the stage" for newcomers to the organization?

8. You have completed an organizational assessment process and identified and prioritized the opportunities for improvement. As part of the process of implementing these opportunities, you need to address potential resistance to change. What are the significant groups within your agency that have the ability to support or impede this change effort, and how can they be made part of the process?

9. You are about to face a change of administration and want to take steps to ensure that your current program of annual organizational self-assessments continues. What actions do you think are critical to efforts to institutionalize such a program so that it can withstand changes of administration?

# Assessment Resources

## Web Sites

American Society for Public Administration: www.aspanet.org

Association of Government Accountants: www.aga.org

Baldrige National Quality Program: www.quality.nist.gov

Center for Performance Measurement, International City/County Management Association (ICMA): www.icma.org

Center for Organizational Development and Leadership, Rutgers University: www.odl.rutgers.edu

City of Coral Springs, Florida (Baldrige page): http://www.coralsprings.org/baldrige/index.cfm

ExpectMore.gov: http://www.whitehouse.gov/omb/expectmore/about.html

Florida Sterling Award: www.floridasterling.com

*Governing Magazine*: www.governing.com

International City/County Management Association: www.icma.org

National Academy of Public Administration: http://www.napawash.org/pc_government_performance/about.html

National Center for Public Productivity: www.ncpp.us

National Governors Association Center for Best Practices: www.nga.org

Quality New Mexico: www.qualitynewmexico.org

Results.gov: http://www.whitehouse.gov/results/

United States Army Armament Research, Development and Engineering Center: http://www.pica.army.mil/PicatinnyPublic/organizations/ardec/index.asp

Washington State Quality Award: www.wsqa.net

# Performance Measurement

Performance measurement is the development and analysis of data to determine the level of operation and achievement. It can be an integral part of addressing the need to quantify efficiency and effectiveness. In an organizational assessment, a strong performance management program can be the source of the data that will be reported in the outcomes category.

Most public sector agencies are quite adept at project specific or technical performance measurement, but less effort has typically gone into determining the appropriate measures for more administrative areas. While the practice of measuring the performance of public sector organizations is not new, performance measurement and program evaluation have become increasingly sophisticated.

Examples of nationally recognized programs that assist agencies and promote the use of performance measurement to assess government include:

■ The American Society for Public Administration's Center for Accountability and Performance, founded in 1996, offers training and resources to government practitioners, academics, and students in promoting performance-based, results-driven government. The resources offered by the Center include training and a performance measurement workbook. The Center maintains a series of case studies illustrating the use of performance measurement in various federal, state, and local government agencies.

■ The National Center for Public Productivity at Rutgers University/Newark, established in 1972, has conducted extensive research into public performance measurement initiatives and provides resources and educational programs for municipalities, state, and federal government agencies and nonprofit organizations. It offers a Web-based proficiency development program that results in a Certificate in Public Performance Measurement. The Center also supports the New Jersey Municipal Performance Measurement System, with over 120 performance indicators.

■ The International City/County Management Association (ICMA) sponsors a Center for Performance Measurement that includes a comprehensive program to collect information on performance measures. It began in 1994 as the Comparative Performance Measurement Consortium, a group of 44 city and county governments that identified a series of performance measures and coordinated that information through ICMA

Now called the Comparative Performance Measurement Program, it has expanded to include over 200 local governments that submit performance measurement data in 15 different service areas. In return, each can use the collective database of information for benchmarking. According to the ICMA Web site, members can customize their benchmarking "based on population, climate, urban density, method of service provision, community demographics" and other criteria.

# Bibliography

Albert, S., and D. Whetten. 1985. Organizational identity. *Research in Organizational Behavior* 7: 263–297.

Altheide, D., and J. Johnson. 1980. *Bureaucratic propaganda*. Boston: Allyn and Bacon.

Ammons, D. 1999. A proper mentality for benchmarking. *Public Administration Review* 59 (2): 105.

Anderson, D., and L. Anderson. 2001. *Beyond change management*. San Francisco: Jossey-Bass.

Arcaro, J. 1998. *The president's Quality Award Program self assessment process for federal, state, and local government*. Boca Raton, FL: CRC Press.

Argyris, C. 1992. *On organizational learning*. Cambridge, MA: Blackwell Publishers.

Argyris, C. 1982. *Reasoning, learning, and action*. San Francisco: Jossey-Bass.

Austin, J., R. Klimoski, and S. Hunt. 1996. Dilemmatics in public sector assessment: A framework for developing and evaluating selection systems. *Human Performance* 9 (3): 177–198.

Aydin, E., and R. E. Rice. 1992. Bringing social worlds together: Computers as catalysts for new interactions in health care organizations. *Journal of Health and Social Behavior* 33 (2): 168–185.

Babicz, G. 2002. Assessing the Baldrige Award. *Quality* 41 (11): 36.

Baldrige National Quality Program. 2003a. *Why apply?* Washington, D.C.: National Institute of Standards and Technology, Department of Commerce.

Baldrige National Quality Program. 2003b. *Getting started*. Washington, D.C.: National Institute of Standards and Technology (NIST), Department of Commerce.

Baldrige National Quality Program. 2007a. *Criteria for performance excellence 2007*. Washington, D.C.: National Institute of Standards and Technology, Department of Commerce.

Baldrige National Quality Program. 2007b. *Criteria for performance excellence in education 2007*. Washington, D.C.: National Institute of Standards and Technology, Department of Commerce.

Baldrige National Quality Program. 2007c. *Criteria for performance excellence in health care 2007*. Washington, D.C.: National Institute of Standards and Technology, Department of Commerce.

Baldrige National Quality Program. 2008. Commerce Secretary Gutierrez joins President Bush in announcing 2008 Baldrige National Quality Awards. Online at: http://www.nist.gov/public_affairs/releases/2008baldrigerecipients.htm

Behn, R. 2003. Why measure performance? Different purposes require different measures. *Public Administration Review* 63 (5): 586–606.

Behn, R. 2008. On why, to improve performance, management is rarely enough. *Bob Behn's Public Management Report* 5 (9). Online at: http://www.hks.harvard.edu/thebehnreport/May2008.pdf

Berman, E. 2002. How useful is performance measurement? *Public Performance & Management Review* 25 (4): 348–351.

Berman, E. 1998. *Productivity in public and non-profit organizations: Strategies and techniques.* Thousand Oaks, CA: Sage Publications.

Berman, E., and J. West. 1995a. TQM in American cities: Hypotheses regarding commitment and impact. *Journal of Public Administration Research & Theory* 5 (2): 213–231.

Berman, E., and J. West. 1995b. Municipal commitment to Total Quality Management: A survey of recent progress. *Public Administration Review* 55 (1): 57–66.

Berman, E., and X.-H. Wang. 2000. Performance measurement in US counties: Capacity for reform. *Public Administration Review* Sept/Oct., 60 (5): 409–434.

Blackburn, R., and B. Rosen. 1993. Total quality and human resource management: Lessons learned from Baldrige award-winning companies. *Academy of Management Executive* 7 (3): 49–67.

Boyne, G. 2006. Strategies for public service turnaround. *Administration and Society* 38 (3): 365–388.

Boyne, G., and A. Chen. 2007. Performance targets and public service improvement. *Journal of Public Administration Research and Theory* 17 (3): 455–477.

Boyne, G., J. Gould-Williams, J. Law, and R. Walker. 2004. Toward the self-evaluating organization? An empirical test of the Wildavsky model. *Public Administration Review* 64 (4): 463–473.

Boyne, G., K. Meier, L. O'Toole Jr., and R. Walker (eds.). 2006. *Public service performance: Perspectives on measurement and management.* New York: Cambridge University Press.

Bozeman, B., and G. Kingsly. 1998. Risk culture in public and private organizations. *Public Administration Review* 58 (2): 109.

Calhoun, J. M. 2002. Using the Baldrige criteria to manage and assess the performance of your organization. *The Journal for Quality & Participation* 25 (2): 45–53.

Carr, D., and I. Littman. 1990. *Excellence in government: Total Quality Management in the 1990s.* Arlington, VA: Coopers and Lybrand.

Cheney, G. 1983. On the various and changing meanings of organizational membership: A field study of organizational identification. *Communication Monographs* 50: 342–362.

Cheney, G., and P. R. Tompkins. 1987. Coming to terms with organizational identification and commitment. *Central States Speech Journal* 38 (1): 1–15.

Chuan, T. K., and L. C. Soon. 2000. A detailed trends analysis of national quality awards world-wide. *Total Quality Management* 11 (8): 1065–1080.

City of Coral Springs, Florida. 2008. *A to Z guide to city and community services.*

Coe, C. 2003. A report card on report cards. *Public Performance Management Review* 27 (2): 53–76.

Coggburn, J., and S. Schneider. 2003a. The quality of management and government performance: An empirical analysis of the American state. *Public Administration Review* 63 (2): 206–213.

Coggburn, J., and S. Schneider. 2003b. The relationship between state government performance and state quality of life. *International Journal of Public Administration* 26 (12): 1337–1354.

Collins, J., and J. Porras. 1994. *Built to last.* New York: Harper Collins.

Committee on Governmental Affairs. 1993. *Report on the Government Performance and Results Act of 1993.* U.S. Senate. Online at: http://www.whitehouse.gov/omb/mgmt-gpra/gprptm.html

Conference Board. 1995. *In pursuit of quality: Views from the leading edge.* New York: The Conference Board.

Connor, P. 1997. Total Quality Management: A selective commentary on its human dimensions. *Public Administration Review* Nov/Dec., 57 (6): 501–509.

Coplin, W., and C. Dwyer. 2000. *Does your government measure up?* Syracuse, NY: Community Benchmarks Program, Maxwell School of Citizenship and Public Affairs, Syracuse University.

Cornin, M. 2004. Continuous improvement in a New York State school district. Unpublished dissertation. Rutgers, The State University of New Jersey, New Brunswick, NJ.

Curkovic, S., S. Menyk, R. Calantone, and R. Handfield. 2000. Validating the Malcolm Baldrige National Quality Award Framework through structural equation modeling. *International Journal of Production Research* 38 (4): 765–791.

DeCarlo, N., and W. K. Sterett. 1995. History of the Malcolm Baldrige National Quality Award. In *Quality in higher education,* ed. B. D. Ruben (pp. 79–96). New Brunswick, NJ: Transaction Publishers.

Deetz, S. 1995. *Transforming communication, transforming business.* New York: Hampton Press.

Dilulio, J., G. Garvey, and D. Kettl. 1993. *Improving government performance: An owner's manual.* Washington, D.C.: Brookings Institution Press.

Douglas, T., and L. Fredenhall. 2004. Evaluating the Deming Management Model of total quality in services. *Decision Sciences* 35 (3): 393–422.

Dubnick, M. 2005. Accountability and the promise of performance. *Public Performance Management Review* 28 (3): 376–417.

Dutton, J., and J. Dukerich. 1991. Keeping an eye on the mirror: Image and identity in organizational adaptation. *Academy of Management Journal* 34 (3): 517–554.

Eagle, K. 2004. The origins and evolution of Charlotte's corporate scorecard. *Government Finance Review* October: 16–22.

Etzione, A. 1964. *Modern organizations*. Englewood Cliffs, NJ: Prentice Hall.

Fernandez, S., and H. Rainey. 2006. Managing successful organizational change in the public sector. *Public Administration Review* March/April: 168–176.

Folz, D. 2004. Service quality and benchmarking the performance of municipal services. *Public Administration Review* March, 64 (2): 209–220.

Fredrickson, D., and H. Fredrickson. 2006. *Measuring the performance of the hollow state*. Washington, D.C.: Georgetown University Press.

Frohman, A. 1997. Igniting organizational change from below: The power of personal initiative. *Organizational Dynamics* Winter: 39–52.

Gabriel, Y. 2000. *Storytelling in organizations*. Oxford, U.K.: Oxford University Press.

Gilliland, M. 2004. Leading a public university: Lessons learned in choosing the possibility of quantum results rather than incremental improvement. *Public Administration Review* 64 (3): 372–377.

Gore, A. 1995. *Common sense government*. New York: Random House.

Government Accounting Office. 1991. *Management practice: U.S. companies improve performance through quality efforts*. (NSAID-91-190). Washington, D.C.

Government Accounting Office. 2004. *Performance budgeting: OMG's program assessment rating tool presents operational challenges for budget and performance integration – statement of Paul S. Posner*. Washington, D.C.

Government Accounting Office. 2008. *Lessons learned for the next administration on using performance information to improve results: Statement of Bernice Steinhardt, director strategic issues*. (GAO-08-1026T). Washington, D.C.

George, S., and A. Weimerskirch. 1994. *Total Quality Management*. New York: John Wiley & Sons.

Haass, R. 1994. *The power to persuade*. Boston: Houghton Mifflin Company.

Haavind, R. 1992. *The road to the Baldrige Award: Quest for total quality*. Stoneham, MA: Butterworth-Heinemann.

Hart, C. L., and C. E. Bogan. 1992. *The Baldrige*. New York: McGraw-Hill.

Heaphy, M. S., and G. F. Gruska. 1995. *The Malcolm Baldrige national quality award: A yardstick for quality growth*. Reading, MA: Addison-Wesley Publishing Company.

Heflin, C. 2007a. Has Coral Springs found the Holy Grail? From Sterling to Baldrige. *Public Sector Digest* Summer.

Heflin, C. 2007b. Has Coral Springs found the Holy Grail? From Sterling to Baldrige. *Public Sector Digest* October.

Heflin, C. 2008. Has Coral Springs found the Holy Grail? From Sterling to Baldrige. *Public Sector Digest* February.

Heinrich, C. 2004. Performance management as administrative reform: Is it improving government performance? *Public Finance and Management* 4 (3): 240–246.

Herzik, E. 1988. Government productivity, effectiveness, and public policy. *Policy Studies Review* 7 (3): 684–691.

Higgs, M., and D. Rowland. 2005. All changes great and small: Exploring approaches to change and its leadership. *Journal of Change Management* 5 (2): 121–151.

Himm, A. 1993. *Does quality work? A review of relevant studies.* New York: The Conference Board.

Hogan, T. J. 1992. The applicability of the Malcolm Baldrige National Quality Award criteria to the evaluation of quality in collegiate administrative services. Unpublished dissertation. Ohio University, Athens, OH.

Holzer, M., and K. Callahan. 1998. *Government at work.* Thousand Oaks, CA: Sage Publications.

Hsieh, A., C. Chou, and C. Chen. 2002. Job standardization and service quality: A closer look at the application of total quality management to the public sector. *Total Quality Management* 13 (7): 899–912.

Hunt, V. 1993. *Quality management for government.* Milwaukee, WI: ASQC Quality Press.

Hutton, D. W. 2000. *From Baldrige to the bottom line.* Milwaukee, WI: ASQ Quality Press.

Immordino, K. 2006. The impact of structured organizational self-assessment processes on issue identification and prioritization. Unpublished dissertation. Rutgers, The State University of New Jersey, New Brunswick, NJ.

Immordino, K. 2009. *Organizational assessment and improvement in the public sector.* New York: Taylor & Francis.

Ingraham, P. (ed.). 2007. *In pursuit of performance: Management systems in state and local government.* Baltimore, MD: Johns Hopkins University Press.

Irr, F., C. Kalnbach, and M. Smith. 2003. The real story behind the commandant's performance challenge. *The Journal for Quality & Participation* Summer: 41–45.

Irvin, J., and J. Stansbury. 2004. Citizen participation in decision making: Is it worth the effort? *Public Administration Review* 64 (1): 55–65.

Jick, T. 1995. Accelerating change for competitive advantage. *Organizational Dynamics,* 14 (1): 77–82.

Kanter, R. M. 1991a. Change: Where to begin. *Harvard Business Review* 69 (4): 8–9.

Kanter, R. M. 1991b. Transcending business boundaries: 12,000 world managers view change. *Harvard Business Review* May/June: 151–164.

Kaplan, R. 2001. Strategic performance measurement and management in nonprofit organizations. *Nonprofit Management and Leadership* 11 (3): 353–370.

Kaplan, R., and D. Norton. 1996. *Balanced scorecard: Translating strategy into action.* Boston: Harvard Business School Press.

Kaplan, R., and D. Norton. 1992. The balanced scorecard—Measures that drive performance. *Harvard Business Review* 70 (1): 71–79.

Katz, D., B. Gutek, R. Kahn, and E. Barton. 1975. *Bureaucratic encounters: A pilot study in the evaluation of government services.* Ann Arbor, MI: University of Michigan Press.

Kearney, R., and E. Berman (eds.). 1999. *Public sector performance: Management, motivation and measurement.* Boulder, CO: Westview Press.

Keehly, P., S. Medlin, S. MacBride, and L. Longmire. 1997. *Benchmarking for best practices in the public sector.* San Francisco: Jossey-Bass.

Kemelgor, B., S. Johnson, and S. Srinivasan. 2000. Forces driving organizational change: A business school perspective. *Journal of Education for Business* January/February: 133–137.

Kravchuk, R., and R. Schack. 1996. Designing effective performance measurement systems under the Government Performance and Results Act. *Public Administration Review* 56 (4): 348–359.

Kulik, T. 1998. *The continuing search for performance excellence.* New York: The Conference Board.

Leith, J. 1997. *Implementing performance measurement in government.* Washington, D.C.: Government Finance Officers Association.

Long, E., and A. L. Franklin. 2004. The paradox of implementing the Government Performance and Results Act: Top-down direction for bottom-up implementation. *Public Administration Review* 64 (3): 309–319.

Mahoney, F. X., and C. G. Thor. 1994. *The TQM trilogy.* New York: American Management Association.

Mehta, P. 2000. President's quality program honors government organizations. *Quality Progress,* 57–62.

Michelson, E. 2006. Approaches to research and development performance assessment in the United States: An evaluation of recent trends. *Science and Public Policy* 33 (8): 546–560.

Neves, J., and B. Nakhai. 1993. The Baldrige Award framework for teaching total quality management. *Journal of Education for Business* 69 (2).

Niven, P. 2005. *Balanced scorecard diagnostics: Maintaining maximum performance.* Hoboken, NJ: John Wiley & Sons.

Niven, P. 2008. *Balanced scorecard: Step by step for government and non-profit agencies.* Hoboken, NJ: John Wiley & Sons.

Nystrom, P., and W. Starbuck (eds.). 1981. *Handbook of organizational design,* Vol. 2. New York: Oxford University Press.

Oman, R., S. Damours, T. Smith, and A. Uscher. 1992. *Management analysis in public organizations.* New York: Quorum Books.

Orr, M., and D. West. 2007. Citizen evaluations of local police: Personal experience or symbolic attitudes? *Administration and Society* 38 (6): 649–668.

Osbourne, D., and T. Gaebler. 1993. *Reinventing government: How the entrepreneurial spirit is transforming the public sector.* New York: Plume.

Pannirselvam, G., and L. Ferguson. 2001. A study of the relationships between the Baldrige categories. *The International Journal of Quality & Reliability* 18 (1): 14.

Pannirselvam, G., S. Siferd, and W. Ruch. 1998. Validation of the Arizona governor's quality award criteria: A test of the Baldrige criteria. *Journal of Operations Management* 16 (5): 529–550.

Pascale, R., M. Millemann, and L. Gioja. 1997. Changing the way we change. *Harvard Business Review* November/December: 127–139.

Pederson, L. 2002. *Performance-oriented management: A practical guide for government agencies.* Vienna, VA: Management Concepts, Inc.

Phillips, J. 2004. An application of the balanced scorecard to public transit system performance assessment. *Transportation Journal* 43 (1): 26–55.

Popovich, M. (ed.). 1998. *Creating high performance government organizations.* San Francisco: Jossey Bass.

Przasnyski, Z., and L. S. Tai. 2002. Stock performance of Malcolm Baldrige National Quality Award winning companies. *Total Quality Management* 13 (4): 475–488.

Purser, R., and J. Petranker. 2005. Unfreezing the future: Exploring the dynamic of time in organizational change. *The Journal of Applied Behavioral Science* 41 (2): 182–203.

Radin, B. 1998. The government performance and results act (GPRA): Hydraheaded monster or flexible management tool? *Public Administration Review* 58 (4): 307.

Raven, B. 1995. The bases of power: Origins and recent developments. In *Foundations of organizational communication,* eds. S. Corman, S. Banks, C. Bantz, and M. Mayer. White Plains, NY: Longman Publishers.

Redburn, F., R. Shea, and T. Buss (eds.). 2008. *Performance management and budgeting: How governments can learn from experience.* Armonk, NY: M.E. Sharpe.

Rogers, E. 1995. Diffusion of innovations. New York: Free Press.

Ruben, B. 1995. *Quality in higher education.* New Brunswick, NJ: Transaction Publishers.

Ruben, B. 2002. Integrating organizational assessment, planning, and improvement: Making organizational self-study and change everyday activities. (Unpublished manuscript.)

Ruben, B. 2004. *Pursuing excellence in higher education.* San Francisco: Jossey-Bass.

Ruben, B. 2005. The center for organizational development at Rutgers University: A case study. *Advances in Developing Human Resources* 7 (3): 368–395.

Ruben, B. 2007a. *Excellence in higher education: a Baldrige-based guide to organizational assessment, improvement and leadership.* Washington, D.C.: National Association of College and University Business Officers.

Ruben, B. 2007b. *Excellence in higher education: A Baldrige-based guide to organizational assessment, improvement and leadership. Workbook and scoring guide.* Washington, D.C.: National Association of College and University Business Officers.

Ruben, B. 2010. Excellence in higher education: A Baldrige-based guide to organizational assessment, improvement, and leadership. Washington, DC: National Association of College and University Business Officers.

Ruben, B., S. Connaughton, K. Immordino, and J. Lopez. 2004. Paper presented at the annual meeting of the National Consortium for Continuous Improvement in Higher Education, Milwaukee, WI, July.

Ruben, B., and K. Immordino. 2006a. *Excellence in the public sector: a Baldrige-based guide to organizational assessment, improvement and leadership.* New Brunswick, NJ: Rutgers University.

Ruben, B., and K. Immordino. 2006b. *Excellence in the public sector: a Baldrige-based guide to organizational assessment, improvement and leadership. Workbook and scoring guide.* New Brunswick, NJ: Rutgers University.

Rusaw, A. 1998. *Transforming the character of public organizations: Techniques for change agents.* Westport, CT: Quorum Books.

Schachter, H. 2007. Does Frederick Taylor's ghost still haunt the halls of government? A look at the concept of governmental efficiency in our time. *Public Administration Review* Sept/Oct: 800–810.

Schein, E. 1980. *Organizational psychology.* Englewood Cliffs, NJ: Prentice-Hall.

Schein, E. 1992. *Organizational culture and leadership.* San Francisco: Jossey-Bass.

Scott, C. 1997. Identification with multiple targets in a geographically dispersed organization. *Management Communication Quarterly* 10 (4): 491–522.

Scott, C., S. Connaughton, H. Diaz-Saenz, K. Maguire, R. Ramirez, B. Richardson, S. Shaw, and D. Morgan. 1999. The impacts of communication and multiple identifications on intent to leave. *Management Communication Quarterly* 12 (3): 400–435.

Scott, S., and V. Lane. 2000. A stakeholder approach to organizational identity. *The Academy of Management Review* 25 (1): 43–62.

Senge, P. 1990. *The fifth discipline: The art and practice of the learning organization.* New York: Doubleday.

Shirks, A., W. B. Weeks, and A. Stein. 2002. Baldrige based quality awards: Veterans Health Administration's 3-year experience. *Quality Management in Health Care* 10 (3): 47–54.

Spechler, J. W. 1993. *Managing quality in America's most admired companies.* San Francisco: Berrett-Koehler Publishers.

Sweeney, S., and J. Charlesworth (eds.). 1963. *Achieving excellence in the public service.* Philadelphia: The American Academy of Political and Social Service.

Syfert, P., N. Elliott, and L. Schumacher. 1998. Charlotte adopts the balanced scorecard. *American City and County* 113 (11): 32.

Van de Ven, A., and M. Poole. 1995. Explaining development and change in organizations. *Academy of Management Review* 20 (3): 510–540.

Van de Ven, A., and M. Poole. 2005. Alternative approaches for studying organizational change. *Organizational Studies* 26 (9): 1377–1404.

Van Wart, M., and L. Dicke (eds.). 2008. *Administrative leadership in the public sector.* Armonk, NY: M.E. Sharpe.

Vokurka, R. J. 2001. The Baldrige at 14. *Journal for Quality and Participation* 24 (2)

Wallace, M., M. Fertig, and E. Schneller (eds.). 2007. *Managing change in the public services.* Malden, MA: Blackwell Publishing.

Walters, L., J. Aydelotte, and J. Miller. 2000. Putting more public in policy analysis. *Public Administration Review* 60 (4): 349.

Weisbord, N. 1987. Productive workplaces. San Francisco: Jossey-Bass.

Willem, A., and M. Buelens. 2007. Knowledge sharing in public sector organizations. *Journal of Public Administration Research and Theory* 17 (4): 581–606.

Wisniewski, M., and M. Donnelly. 1996. Measuring service quality in the public sector: The potential for SERVQUAL. *Total Quality Management* 7 (4): 357–365.

Witherspoon, P. 1997. *Communicating leadership.* Boston: Allyn and Bacon.

Yang, K., and K. Callahan. 2007. Citizen involvement efforts and bureaucratic responsiveness: Participatory values, stakeholder pressures, and administrative practicality. *Public Administration Review* March/April: 249–264.

Younis, T. 1997. Customers' expectations of public sector services: Does quality have its limits? *Total Quality Management* 8 (4): 115–129.

Younis, T. 2007. Army facility wins national quality award. Online at: www. GovernmentExecutive.com (accessed December 10, 2007).

Younis, T. 2008. Far-sighted: Long range focus allows city government to celebrate Baldrige recognition. Online at: www.qualityprogress.com (accessed September 22, 2008).

# Interviews

Jeffrey Weinrach, Director, Quality New Mexico.

Mark Tucci, Director, Human Resources, New Jersey Department of Environmental Protection.

Alfred Brenner, Director of the Division of Support Services, New Jersey Department of Transportation.

David Kuhn, Director of the Division of Local Aid, New Jersey Department of Transportation.

Brad Sampson, Army Armament Research Development and Engineering Center.

Susan Grant, Director of Human Resources, City of Coral Springs, Florida.

Joseph Genovay, Manager, New Jersey Department of Environmental Protection.

Michael Hanson, Office of the Governor, State of Utah.

# Email Correspondence

Susan Fourney, Managing Editor, *Governing Magazine* (March 12, 2007).

Brad Sampson, Army Armament Research Development and Engineering Center.

Michael Hanson, Office of the Governor, State of Utah.

Maria Fuentes-Archilla, Public Information Officer, City of Coral Springs, Florida.
Jeffrey Weinrach, Director, Quality New Mexico.

## Webcast

International City and County Management Association (2008) Why the Baldrige Quality Model Works in Local Government, January 24, 2008.

# Index